WHOLENESS & FREEDOM CONFERENCE

RESTORING LIVES
EQUIPPING PEOPLE

Acknowledgement

Firstly, I would like to express my deepest gratitude to our Lord Jesus, for this wonderful ministry of healing the broken hearted and setting captives free. Without the work of the Holy Spirit, it is impossible to see people's lives transformed. I consider this ministry a God given opportunity and privilege to be a blessing to people.

Every testimony leaves me in awe of God's unfailing love, compassion and mercy, that never ceases to lift people up from the depths of depravity and from the bondages that they have been in, and to see Him accept them as He would accept His own Son, the Lord Jesus Christ.

I am indebted to all the Pastors and Christian leaders who have supported us and have been open to embrace this ministry for their congregations and cities.

I thank all those who have given their testimonies, and shared openly what God has done in their lives. To protect their privacy and dignity, we have deliberately not mentioned their names in this booklet.

I am also grateful to my wife, *Annie D'Monte,* for standing with me during the most challenging of times, and as we've seen God touch and transform lives for the last 30+ years of ministry.

I wish to express my sincere thanks to *Rohit Jadhav,* and all those who helped in making this book possible. Particularly *Esther S. Rajkumar,* who is known for her editing skills and for keeping deadlines, and who worked with such dedication to make this possible.

Last but not the least, God has blessed us with an amazing Ministry Team; all of whom carry our commitment and the Lord's compassion to the people they minister to. This Team travels and works so relentlessly at every given opportunity. We are able to conduct each of these schools for 100+ people because of their voluntary support.

Your fellow brother in Christ,
Victor D'Monte

Table Of Contents

CHAPTER 1

Foundations To
The Healing & Deliverance Ministry

1.1 Creation and the Fall

a. God made the Heavens and the Earth. *(Genesis 1:1, Colossians 1:16)*

b. <u>Spiritual Realm</u> *(Hebrews 1:14)*
    The Spiritual Realm is populated by angels, and these angels were created by God to serve Him and to minister on His behalf.
    Some of these angels have names, and they are given certain responsibilities:
    Gabriel - *Daniel 9:21, Luke 1:19 & 26*
    Michael - *Daniel 10:13*
    Lucifer - *Isaiah 14 & 28*

c. Rebellion in Heaven, and Satan loses his place of authority.
    (Revelation 12:7-9, Luke 10:18, Isaiah 14:12-23, Ezekiel 28:11-19, Jude 6)

d. <u>Earthly Realm</u>
    God created man to have dominion over the Earth. *(Genesis 1:26)*

e. God gave man one instruction. *(Genesis 2:16-17, II Corinthians 4:4)*

f. Man's disobedience resulted in sin, sickness and disease. *(Ephesians 2:2, Acts 10:38, I Peter 5:8)*

Notes:

1.2 God's Solution is to rescue man from that place of captivity (*Genesis 3:15, 1 John 3:8, Luke 10:19*)

Isaiah 53:5
"But He was wounded for our transgressions, He was bruised for our iniquities; the chastisement for our peace was upon Him, and by His stripes we are healed."

Matthew 8:17
"That it might be fulfilled which was spoken by Isaiah the prophet, saying: 'He Himself took our infirmities and bore our sicknesses'."

Romans 4:15
"Because the law brings about wrath; for where there is no law there is no transgression."

1.3 The two ways in which the Gifts of Healing operate

a. <u>In an evangelistic setting, in order to lead people to Christ.</u>
Matthew 11:20-21
"Then He began to rebuke the cities in which most of His mighty works had been done, because they did not repent: 'Woe to you, Chorazin! Woe to you, Bethsaida! For if the mighty works which were done in you had been done in Tyre and Sidon, they would have repented long ago in sackcloth and ashes."

b. <u>Within the Body of Christ – the Church – so that people will live in divine health.</u>
James 5:16
"Confess your trespasses to one another, and pray for one another, that you may be healed. The effective, fervent prayer of a righteous man avails much."

There is a difference between the confession of our sin before God, so that we can receive forgiveness.
(*I John 1:9*) and the confession which is for our healing (*James 5:16*)

The promises of God came into glorious completion on Earth as man agreed with God.
(*II Corinthians 1:20*)

Notes:

CHAPTER 2

Introduction To The Healing Ministry

2.1 God created man to be Whole and Healthy

a. Man was created to function as a healthy being - Spirit, Soul and Body. (*Genesis 2:7, I Thessalonians 5:23*)

b. Before the fall, man was secure in a sinless existence, where there was no decay or death. After the fall, sin caused damage and disorder (*Genesis 4, Genesis 5:5, Genesis 6:3*). The outworking of this spiritual death is seen in the next generation, where Cain kills Abel.

2.2 What do we mean by Healing or Wholeness?

The dictionary meaning of 'wholeness' is 'an undivided or unbroken completeness; or totality with nothing wanting; a state of robust and good health'.

a. To restore Godly order.
b. To make whole and healthy.
c. To restore to health or good condition.
d. To replace turmoil and confusion with peace.
e. To deal with blockages that hinder the sanctification process.

Notes:

2.3 Fruits and Roots

a. Injury to one of the constituent parts of man can cause pain to the other parts, and possible malfunction of the whole being.

b. Recognising the malfunction of any part of our being is the first step to appropriating the healing that Jesus won on the cross. (We could be sick due to the problems we have in our spirit, soul, body, or it could also be generational)

2.4 The Nature of Man

God has made man a complex being. It is helpful to consider the nature of man by looking at three areas - spirit, soul and body.

I Thessalonians 5:23
"May God himself, the God of peace, sanctify you through and through. May your whole spirit, soul and body be kept blameless at the coming of our Lord Jesus Christ."

a. The Human Spirit

- The human spirit is that part of our being with which we relate to God. *(John 4:24)*
- Our human spirit should be fed, and grow strong as we mature in body and soul. *(Luke 1:80, 2:40)*
- The function of the human spirit is primarily to receive and communicate life to our body and soul. *(James 2:26, Luke 23:46)*
- The human spirit receives "new birth". *(John 3:16)*

b. The Soul

i. <u>The Will</u>
- God created us with a free-will; the ability to choose right or wrong. *(Genesis 2:17)*
- The importance of making choices is outlined in the scripture. *(Deuteronomy 30:19)*
- We must be aware of our will before we can surrender it to God's Will. *(Luke 22:42)*

ii. <u>The Mind</u>
- We conceive an idea in our mind, and this leads to, us accordingly speaking out words or behaving in a particular way. *(James 1:15, Psalm 7:14, Isaiah 59:7-8, Genesis 6:5-6)*

Notes:

- We can decide to set our mind on spiritual things. *(Romans 8:5-6)*
- We must work at renewing our mind. *(Romans 12:2)*
- The mind needs to be fed with the correct diet. *(Philippians 4:8-9)*

iii. The Emotions

- God has emotions, and we are made in His Image. *(Exodus 34:5, Galatians 5:22-23)*
- Jesus demonstrates the Emotions of God. *(John 11:35, Matthew 9:36)*
- Emotional training and nurturing are essential to the emotional well-being of a person.
- Right emotions can be expressed at the wrong time or in the wrong way.
- Emotions can be used to manipulate or abuse others.

c. The Body

The body we have is a wonderful machine, and like any other machine it needs a driver. The one who drives this machine is the Soul. The Soul is the interface between the body and spirit.

- The material (carnal) part of man. *(Romans 8:6)*
- Self healing to a certain extent.
- The body often reflects what is going on in the inner man. i.e. If you are happy or sad, your body reflects that likewise.

2.5 The Healing Ministry of Jesus

a. Encounters of Inner Healing

- The paralysed man. *(Luke 5:17-25)*
- The woman at the well. *(John 4:1-42)*
- The woman with the issue of blood. *(Luke 8:42-48)*
- The woman in adultery. *(John 8:1-11)*
- Simon Peter. *(John 21:15-19)*

b. Some of the Physical Healings

- The man with a skin-disease. *(Matthew 8:1-4, Mark 1:40-45, Luke 5:12-16)*
- The man with a paralysed hand. *(Matthew 12:9-14, Mark 3:1-6, Luke 6:6-11)*
- The Roman Officer's servant. *(Matthew 8:5-13, Luke 7:1-10)*
- Jairus' daughter. *(Matthew 9:18-26, Mark 5:21-43, Luke 8:40-56)*

Notes:

c. <u>Ministry of Deliverance</u>
- The unclean spirit in the Synagogue. *(Mark 1:21-28, Luke 4:31-37)*
- The dumb demoniac. *(Matthew 9:32)*
- The blind and dumb demoniac. *(Matthew 12:22-29, Mark 3:22-27, Luke 11:14-23)*
- The epileptic boy. *(Matthew 17:14-21, Mark 9:14-29, Luke 9:37-43)*
- The Gerasene demoniac. *(Matthew 8:28-34, Mark 5:1-20, Luke 8:26-39)*
- The Syro-Phoenician woman's daughter. *(Matthew 15:21-28, Mark 7:24-30)*
- The woman with a spirit of infirmity. *(Luke 13:10-17)*
- Simon Peter's mother-in-law. *(Luke 4:38-39)*
- General references to the Deliverance Ministry. *(Matthew 4:24, 8:16; Mark 1:32-34, 39, 3:11 and 6:13, Luke 4:41, 6:18, 7:21, Acts 5:16, 8:7)*
- Commission to cast out demons. *(Matthew 10:8, Mark 3:15, 6:7, 13 & 16:17-18, Luke 9:1-2)*

Notes:

Testimonies For The Healing Ministry Of Jesus

TESTIMONY I

My father had always been a very healthy man. But he suddenly took ill one day and after spending 24 hours in a hospital, he passed away. This happened in 1997, and it came as a big shock to me. 14 years later, I was living my life, but I was still affected by the shock of my father's death all those years ago… though I didn't realize it's full extent.

In the ensuing years, I developed severe heart palpitations that would be set off by normal everyday life activities… for example, if the telephone rang, or someone rang our doorbell, it would set my heart racing. Things kept getting worse as I started to get irritable, physically weak, and began losing sleep at night. And it further worsened to the point that if people were talking in the room I was in, to me it felt like they were shouting, and I couldn't take it. I met several doctors, none of whom could find anything wrong. One even went to the extent of saying that this was all in my imagination, which really upset me. Finally, in 2004 I was diagnosed with MVP - Mitral Valve Prolapse, a condition where one of the valves in my heart was prolapsed. In fact, just before I had met the doctor who diagnosed this, I was rushed to the hospital since I had suffered a panic attack; its symptoms are very similar to a heart attack.

So, after the diagnosis, I was put on a medicine called a 'beta blocker' which had to be taken every morning. Though I was pretty regular at taking my medicine, there were times I would sometimes forget with the busyness of everyday life, and by 4 PM I would suffer from severe palpitations, which would subside once I took the medication. Around this time I started travelling a lot, and flying was absolutely terrible, since being airborne my chest would contract and there were many a time I thought I wouldn't make it through that flight.

But during my time of ministry, the ministry team member began to pray for the intense trauma I had suffered, and God came and I could begin to feel God touching me and doing something on my heart. I was healed! Since then I've never had to take that medicine ever. I still feel reluctant to fly, but experience no pain or any problem. I thank God for completely healing me. What a great experience. Thank you, Victor and Ann, and everyone at Adonai, for this ministry that has impacted so many lives.

God is absolutely Awesome!

(This is the testimony of Pastor Basil D'Souza, who is the Senior Pastor at Covenant Blessings Church, in Thane, Maharashtra, who has given his consent to have his name included with the testimony)

TESTIMONY II

Soon after our marriage in October 1983, I was suddenly hit by a rash that initially began on my chest as four small circular spots. This happened on our honeymoon. And to our shock, within a month this vicious rash had spread all over my body, and was also accompanied by an incessant itch. As I would scratch, there would be incessant flaking of my skin, from my head to my toes. The skin specialist diagnosed it as psoriasis, and added for good measure, that it was known as 'a healthy man's disease'. And, there was no real treatment for this at that time. So, for the next 26 years, we tried different treatments: homeopathy, ayurveda, allopathy, and a strict restrictive vegetarian diet. You name it, we tried it; hydrotherapy, internal cleansing, oil massages, etc. I would go through seasonal ups and downs, and my skin would sometimes clear completely. But, those times were short-lived.

Gradually the bandwidth of my diet also grew increasingly narrower. My overall health began to deteriorate, until in 1996, when I discovered that this condition now had affected my bones, and was now known as psoriatic arthritis. My pain was compounded.

My beloved wife, and our two children, along with members of our Churches, and many others, prayed and loved me dearly through these agonizing times. I am ever so grateful to them for this. But, there seemed no solution in sight: Prayer; Faith in the Word. I tried it all.

I had reached a point where I began to experience difficulty in walking. My back was bent with my spine locking my upper back into an ageing curve. I had some respite when a doctor recommended a slew of vitamins. But the flaking of my skin continued, and the pain in my joints, though less, was still there. Then a Christian doctor recommended an allopathic tablet called 'metatextrate'. That gave me further relief. But the flaking of the skin continued…until I attended the Adonai Healing and Deliverance Conference in Bangalore, in April 2009.

God dealt with many issues in my life. During the time of my personal ministry, God took me to that place when I was 6 years old (I was being ministered to when I was 60). I had confessed to sexual sin in my pre-christian life, which I had dealt with then. And while being ministered to, the ministry team member asked me when it had started. I told him it had begun when I was in boarding school, and he was shocked to know that I had gone to a boarding school when I was 6 years old. My elder brothers and sister had been there to watch over me, but they couldn't have given me the love, affirmation, protection and direction that I had needed as a 6-year-old from my parent. To cut a long story short, I had to forgive my parents. I realized that they had meant well when they had decided to send me to boarding school where my elder siblings attended, so that I would be educated, and yet they had fallen short of God's standards.

The root of my problem, which was explained to me, was the lack of the Father's Love. I was left vulnerable and insecure. Lovingly, and finding myself suddenly weeping, I prayed a prayer, forgiving my parents.

After the Healing and Deliverance Conference, I returned to Mumbai, in the sweltering heat of April. Because of the heat, I drank lassi and chass and ate things like cashew nuts, etc. All of these would have earlier resulted in a lot of skin flaking and joint pains. But this time, nothing of that sort happened.

It's been 6 years since then, and there has been virtually no flaking of skin and no joint pains. I can eat many more things. If anything, I have a flip problem - I'm developing a paunch!
Glory to Jesus, my Healer and Deliverer.

(This is the testimony of Pastor David Fernandes, who is the Senior Pastor at Living Word Church, in Mumbai, Maharashtra, who has given his consent to have his name included with the testimony

TESTIMONY III

What I experienced during the Healing and Deliverance Conference and what I received from God during this Conference is something that I'm still trying to grasp... I left as a precious child of God!

God continued to work in me even on the last day! On the last day, for some strange reason, I was feeling very incomplete. We had the Breaking of Bread, and as everyone was worshipping, I remember Pastor Victor asking if there was someone who felt any disturbance in their stomach. I thought I had been healed of my stomach problems, but, as soon as Pastor said that, I felt such a churning in my stomach. Initially, I thought it was just a 'feeling', but then the churning got so intense and I knew something was happening. Before I realized it, I fell to the ground. It was such an amazing experience, and I knew right then that I was being healed; Jesus was with me!

For many years I had been suffering from stomach and digestive related problems. I had been to the doctor at various times, and was told to avoid a lot of food like dairy products, wheat, beans, maida, oily foods, etc. Finally the doctor gave up and said I had a very sensitive stomach; I had to be very careful about what I ate and how much I ate.

Up until then, travelling had always been a problem with regards to food. But, during the Healing and Deliverance Conference I had no major problem, and on the last day, God just blew my mind by choosing to heal me even in this area. What an amazing gift!

In the past, I thought I would never be able to fast and pray because of my stomach condition, but now I know I can. I can now also enjoy food without being scared of what may happen next. My stomach doesn't have that heavy / uneasy feeling, and the bloating has all gone. All these years I was always known as the girl with the bad stomach... Haha! But now my friends and family are so surprised with my diet :)

It's been 2 years since I've attended the Healing and Deliverance Conference and it has been such a joy to be able to share my testimony with them. And every time a doubt or negative thought tries to creep in, I immediately go back and hold onto the truth, and remember what was shared at the Conference. I have also learnt to take care of my health and am learning to discipline my life in the areas of my eating habits and exercise.

I am just so thrilled that God chose to touch me, and this is something that I will hold onto for the rest of my life. I am so humbled by His Love.

It has been a joyous and challenging journey, and I'm so thankful and blessed to have done the Healing and Deliverance Conference. THANK YOU!

TESTIMONY IV

I had blisters on my palate, and during my time of ministry, I was healed of this. As I dealt with the idolatry I had practiced in the past, I sought forgiveness from God and renounced all the forms of idol worship I had participated in, and without even praying for this particular healing, God so faithfully healed me.

Principles Of Acceptance

3.1 Definitions

a. 'Acceptance' means 'pleasing, adequate, to regard with favour'. The best definition for acceptance is 'Love in Action'.
b. There are two kinds of Acceptance:
   i. Duty Acceptance
   ii. Wholehearted Acceptance
c. God accepts us not because He has to, but because He wants to. *(Isaiah 49:15-16, Psalm 27:10)*

3.2 The Character of God

a. He is our 'Abba' - a word which conveys intimacy and a personal relationship. *(Romans 8:15)*
b. God is our Loving Father who welcomes each one of us. *(Luke 15, Romans 10:15)*
c. God is our Father who accepts us unconditionally. *(Matthew 8:2-3, Ephesians 1:6)*

3.3 The Character of Man

a. We are made in the Image of God. *(Genesis 1:25-31)*
b. Everything that God created was good. But after God created man the Bible says, "indeed it was very good."
c. In the garden, both Adam and Eve knew that they were accepted.

Notes:

d. God wants us to unconditionally accept each other.
Romans 15:7
"Accept one another, then, just as Christ accepted you, in order to bring praise to God."

3.4 The Enemy's Work and its Consequences

a. Satan sowed doubts about God's acceptance. *(Genesis 3:1)*
b. After the fall, there was the loss of peace and security for all of mankind. *(Genesis 3:16-19)*
   From the moment man fell, he became unacceptable to one another. They both lost that place of openness towards each other.
c. God's plan was to re-establish peace and security through the seed of the woman.
   (Genesis 3:14-15)

3.5 How we Learn about Acceptance

a. <u>Our earthly family is meant to model Kingdom Family</u>
   i. The basic needs of man are food and shelter - physical and spiritual.

   ii. The Biblical truths about parents.
   - They are to be a Godly example. *(Ephesians 4:29, 32)*
   - To give unconditional love. *(Titus 2:4)*
   - To provide for their children. *(II Corinthians 12:14)*
   - To train and discipline their children when necessary. *(Ephesians 6:4)*
   - Parents should spend time with their children. *(Matthew 17:15-16)*

b. <u>Reality of family life</u>
   i. Parents and their behaviours root in us beliefs about who God is, and who we are.
   ii. Distant and abusive parents can lead us to having thoughts of, *"I am worthless and of no value"*, and *"God couldn't care about me or is out to hurt me."*
   iii. Harsh or violent parents can lead to thoughts of, *"I am bad and will always get punished"* and *"God has a big stick to chastise me. He will not show me any mercy."*
   iv. Controlling or unpredictable parents can lead to thoughts of, *"I am unable to think for myself or make any decisions. I'm sure to get it wrong"*, and *"God can never be pleased."*

Notes:

3.6 **Accepting God**

a. Wrong beliefs about God formed through life's experiences, need to be acknowledged and brought into line with the truth of who He is. *(Exodus 34:6-7, Romans 12:2)*
b. Accepting God for Who He really is, helps us to accept ourselves and others. *(John 15:12)*

3.7 **Accepting Ourselves**

a. To accept others we must first accept ourselves. *(Matthew 22:3, Psalm 139, Luke 10:27)*
b. God sees us as 'His special creation'. *(Isaiah 49:15-16, Deuteronomy 26:18, John 10:29)*
c. We are unconditionally accepted, even in our sinful state. *(Luke 6:35, Hebrews 12:10)*

3.8 **Accepting Others**

a. The spiritual law of sowing and reaping also applies to acceptance. *(Galatians 6:7)*
b. Accepting others is a requirement of Kingdom living - *(Colossians 3:12)*
i. Honour (value) all men. *(I Peter 2:17)*
ii. Accept one another. *(Romans 15:7)*

Notes:

Testimonies For Acceptance

TESTIMONY I

I was born into a Christian family, but I hardly knew anything about God and His Love for me. It was at the Healing and Deliverance Conference that I came to know God in a very new way. In the past, I used to blame myself and feel guilty because of the sins I had committed. But, during my time in ministry, I was able to let go of the bitterness, and forgive - both others and myself.

TESTIMONY II

From the earliest of times, I remember that there was always tension between my parents, and so there were constant fights where they would abuse, accuse and threaten each other. And since I shared the same birthday as my father, this only angered my mother further; she would tell me that I was born on the most cursed day and she would vent the frustration that she felt towards my father onto me.

Another thing was that my grades weren't too good, and this only increased my mother's frustration, since she considered education the most important thing in life. And so in her anger, she would tell me I was a mistake, I wasn't good enough to be part of the family, I wasn't their son and was probably exchanged at the hospital with a child from the slums. All this hurt me deeply. I hated my mother and even ran away from home a couple of times.

And I also had to face my father's anger; I remember being terrified of him till my late teens. I have received plenty of beatings from him, and his angry face was deeply imprinted in my childhood. In his anger, he would also call me names and hurl abuses. I felt humiliated and ashamed, and wished I was anybody else but myself.

I felt I was a burden to my family, and even came to the point where I thought I would end my life, but fortunately, I didn't go through with it. And so I grew up as an angry teenager. I would provoke people just so I could fight with them. I also slowly got deeply tangled with pornography. Since I hated my reality, I used porn to escape into fantasy, where I thought I was getting pleasure and love through the only way I now knew.

There was a time when I did allow God to come and help me, but this lasted only for 3-4 months, and

I was again hooked onto porn. My studies also suffered terribly, and I failed every exam, leading to me repeatedly flunking for 6 years. I thought my life was an example of what a cursed life was. I then got into a relationship with a girl, and for the next 2 years, I invested myself wholeheartedly into this relationship, only to later learn that she was going out with my close friend behind my back. I was so overwhelmed with emotions that I got out of the house and just kept walking. I had walked for more than an hour, and then found myself in some distant place. I felt something on the inside of me had died; there was so much sorrow that I couldn't feel anything else.

Around the same time I began to vomit and develop pain in the lower right side of my stomach. I neglected this, but as things only worsened, my parents forcefully took me for surgery, where a half-hour surgery turned into a four-hour surgery; my appendix had ruptured, and when they pierced my stomach, all they found was pus. They had to make an opening and wash my organs after removing the pus; this was almost the end of me. My recovery was also frightening, and it was only God's grace that I survived. My parents were traumatized to see me in this condition, and they decided I needed a chance to have a fresh start.

And that was how I came to Bangalore. A friend of mine introduced me to Adonai Church, and I did the Encounter with God after a year. At the Encounter what touched me the most was the Love of the Father. I experienced His acceptance and felt the grip of condemnation and guilt loosen. Realizing I needed more, I did the Healing and Deliverance Conference. The teachings were a revelation of who God was, and it exposed the lies I had believed my whole life. The Love of the Father flooded my heart with such joy and life. The teachings on 'Rejection' and 'Emotional Pain' helped me to understand how I had lacked acceptance, and out of that lack came my addiction to porn.

I saw, how I had responded with rebellion and hardened my emotions and suppressed my tears.

I tasted the Forgiveness and Love of God, and then felt love towards my family. I was so encouraged and filled with passion to live for God from that day. It was so much easier now to forgive, love and show kindness. I enjoyed reading and studying the Word of God, and delighted in spending time with Him. I saw a change in my attitude towards my parents. I found purpose in living and pursuing the Kingdom of God. And as I continued to grow I was drawn to pray for my family, and today I have the joy of having seen my father, mother and sister receive Jesus as their Saviour!

The blessings I have seen are just a testimony of God as our Father who provides without any lack. Today, I live without any addictions, healed in my body, made whole in my mind and emotions. I am blessed and have been married since 2014 to a beautiful God-fearing girl, have great in-laws, have a great job, a house of my own, a car and 2 bikes. And I am blessed to have the fellowship I enjoy with God and others – it is a taste of Heaven on Earth. It is indeed so amazing to see God's Power touch people's lives, healing and setting them free. From sinner to saint, captivity to freedom, brokenness to being whole!

CHAPTER 4

Dealing With Rejection

4.1 God's Original Plan

a. God created Adam and Eve and placed them in Eden, a place of love, joy, gladness, thanksgiving, and the voice of singing. ***Isaiah 51:3 (NKJV)***

b. Man was created to live in an atmosphere of unconditional love, unconditional acceptance and a place of security (a place of belonging). The atmosphere is very important. This was the covering the Father, Son and Holy Spirit provided for mankind.

Mankind was in unity with God. All his needs were provided for by God, and he was made in the Image of God.

Genesis 1:26-27
"Then God said, 'Let Us make man in Our image, according to Our likeness; let them have dominion over the fish of the sea, over the birds of the air, and over the cattle, over all the earth and over every creeping thing that creeps on the earth'. So, God created man in His own image; in the image of God He created him; male and female He created them."

Notes:

c. Man's disobedience brought him out of this covering.
    The enemy appeared to Eve, questioned the Word of God, and sowed lies in Eve. *(Genesis 3)*

d. The Characteristics of the Enemy.
    John 10:10
    "The thief does not come except to steal, and to kill, and to destroy."

e. Rejection begins with a sense of lack. e.g. Lack of love, lack of acceptance. A deficit of love leaves man feeling rejected.

f. God's way of providing love, acceptance and security is through parenting. Parents are to nurture their children in love, show them total acceptance and provide security.

g. Lucifer's sin caused him to be rejected from God's presence.
    Satan is a rejected being, and he is looking for company.

h. <u>There are 3 basic needs in each of us:</u>
    i.   The need to be loved
    ii. The need to be accepted
    iii. The need for identity

4.2 The fallen world is filled with rejection

a. The world system we live in is based on either conditional acceptance or rejection.
b. All relationships make us vulnerable to the possibility of rejection.
c. Rejection leads to the fear of rejection.
d. When others reject us, we either agree with them and self-reject ourself, or disagree and go into rebellion.

4.3 Roots of Rejection

a. At conception, birth, gender
b. Our character and looks

Notes:

c. Adoption, fostering or abandonment

d. Sibling rivalry

e. Family pressures

f. Hospitalisation

g. Separation from parents or death of loved ones

h. Deformity or disability of a family member

i. Our achievements and failures

j. Consequences of poverty

k. Culture or language

l. Broken relationship/Divorce

m. Breakdown of family

4.4 Understanding My Response to Rejection

a. <u>Reality</u>
    i. Being real about my past and how I have received rejection, even if I don't feel the pain of the memories. *(John 8:32)*
    ii. Acknowledging that the past rejection has had an effect on me today is necessary.
    iii. Realising that the behaviour which seems to be "natural" when I am hurt, may well be sin.

Following are some of the sinful attitudes and behaviours of people who have suffered rejection:
- Anger
- Judgement and criticism
- Control
- People pleasing
- Unreality
- Perfectionism and striving
- Self-deception

Notes:

b. <u>My Behaviour is My Responsibility</u>
  i. People who have not felt accepted, and who do not have a sense of belonging, are insecure. They often try to make themselves feel more secure by behaving in certain ways; it is as if they try to cover the insecure place in their own strength. *(Genesis 3:7)*
  ii. These behaviours become so much a part of the individual's life, that they may have difficulty in believing that they can actually behave differently. The truth is that God is our defence and security, and so, to defend ourselves is taking His Place, and is therefore sin.
  iii. We need to take responsibility for our sinful behaviour, and repent. *(I John 1:8-9)*
  iv. Healing of the pain of rejection can then follow. *(James 5:16)*

c. <u>The Way Forward</u>
  i. Understand and acknowledge the reality of how parenting and other situations have affected me. *(Psalm 27:10)*
  ii. I need to start being accountable for my own sinful behaviour.
  iii. Forgive those who have not treated me according to God's Plan for my life, irrespective of whether I recognise the hurt it has caused me or not. *(Matthew 18:22)*
  iv. Recognise and release the pain; this is necessary for healing.
  v. Recognise that Jesus took my rejection on the cross, in order to give me His Acceptance.
  vi. I need to make a choice to live under God's covering of unconditional love, total acceptance and security.

I Choose To Reject The Lie And Accept The Truth

I Am No Longer A Product Of The Past But A Product Of The Cross

Notes:

Testimonies For Rejection

TESTIMONY I

I came here with a lot of rejection, pain, hurt, unforgiveness and sin in my life. I was rejected by my parents because they wanted a boy, and I was born a girl. My mother tried to abort me many times and I was born premature. But God had a plan and purpose for my life. When I was a six-month-old baby my family gave me up for adoption. And the parents who adopted me used to tell everyone that I wasn't their child and was adopted. This caused me much pain and made me feel rejected. I felt that there was no one who loved me, no one who cared for me.

During my time of ministry, I was delivered from the trauma, pain and guilt. What an amazing God He is! I was healed of the wounding and pain, and felt such a relief. I now know I have a Heavenly Father who loves me unconditionally; He just pours out His Love. I used to feel like a bird who was caught in a cage, but today I am free!

TESTIMONY II

I envied my sister. She was beautiful, tall and could make heads turn when she walked into a room. I was jealous of her good looks and the way people liked her because she was so easy to get along with. Compared to her, I felt I was gawky and lanky. My mother always favoured my sister, and that made me hate her even more! Coming to the Encounter with God changed the way I looked at myself. I realized that I was precious in God's Eyes; I was a 'masterpiece'! I now know that every fiber in my being is loved by my Heavenly Father. I was able to forgive my mother and myself. Today I feel so light-hearted, that I could almost fly!

TESTIMONY III

I've always wondered why my biological mother rejected me. She had given me up for adoption. And I love my parents who adopted me; but this question always nagged me. I know I look nothing like my adoptive parents, and there were times when comments which were passed casually about this would really hurt me. I had no idea what the Encounter with God was going to be about, but as each session began, I was overwhelmed; I could relate to each topic. I enjoyed my personal ministry and was able to forgive my biological mother and deal with rejection. I feel like a weight has been lifted off me. Thank you!

TESTIMONY IV

The Healing and Deliverance Conference has helped me to feel again. I was hurt in the area of relationships and also came from a family where there was a lot of rejection and abuse. As a result, I built walls around me-emotionally and had a tough time connecting with my family. My father was also abusive, and though I thought I had forgiven him, it's only now at the Conference that I was able to forgive him wholeheartedly and also bless him as I prayed for him. Today, I am healed and see those walls are broken. For 10 years I had also struggled with sexual sins; lust and pornography were strongholds in my life. Now I can say with the assurance of Christ, that I am healed and delivered from the spirits of lust, fear and timidity.

CHAPTER 5

Principles Of Forgiveness

5.1 Why is Forgiveness so important?

a. The Heart of God is to forgive. *(Numbers 14:18, Psalm 51, I John 1:9)*
    The two aspects of God's Forgiveness are:
    Isaiah 43:25
    "I, even I, am he who <u>blots out your transgressions</u>, for my own sake, and <u>remembers your sins</u>
    <u>no more</u>."

    Isaiah 1:18
    "'Come now, let us settle the matter,' says the Lord. 'Though your sins are like scarlet, they shall be
    as white as snow; though they are red as crimson, they shall be like wool'."

b. Jesus taught His disciples that in the Kingdom of God, forgiveness, is a way of life.
    Unless we forgive others we are not able to receive forgiveness for ourselves. *(Matthew 18:21-35,*
    Matthew 6:12)
c. Jesus not only taught about forgiveness, He demonstrated it to the greatest extent - giving His Life
    on the Cross. *(Luke 23:33, 34)*
d. Forgiveness is often a major key in the process of healing.

Notes:

Forgiveness Is To 'Untie And Release'

5.2 Forgiveness means

a. Being willing to acknowledge what is really in our hearts when we have been sinned against. *(Jeremiah 17:9-10)*
b. Separating the sin from the sinner. *(John 8:1-11)*
c. Choosing mercy and not judgement. *(James 2:12-13)*
d. Not waiting to forgive until we feel forgiveness is deserved. *(Luke 23:34, Acts 7:60)*
e. Becoming an agent of forgiveness instead of staying a victim.
f. Giving to God our "right of revenge". *(Romans 12:17-21)*

Forgiveness Is For Your Benefit

5.3 Who do we need to Forgive?

a. Others *(Matthew 6:15)*
b. Ourselves *(Mark 11:25; Colossians 3:13)*
c. God *(Jonah 4:1-4)*

The One You Resent Is The One You Resemble

5.4 How do we Forgive?

a. Isaiah 43:25

   "I, even I, am he who blots out your transgressions, for my own sake, and remembers your sins no more."

   i. Blotting out - by forgiving.
   ii. Remembering no more - making a choice to not remember.
b. Realise that forgiveness is an act of obedience to the command of Jesus - it is a choice of will.

Notes:

c. Continue to forgive until the wounding is healed.

d. Recognise and repent of any bitterness, anger, or hatred towards those who have offended us.

e. Acknowledge and repent of any judgements we have made, realising that when we sow a judgement we will reap the effect. *(Matthew 7:1-2)*

Say It, Mean It, Feel It

5.5 Unforgiveness leads to Judgement

a. Bitter Root Judgement.

b. People who have been hurt often make judgements against those who have hurt them. Judgements are authoritative, sinful, and condemning pronouncements against others.

c. God's unchanginsg laws mean that if I sow a judgement I will reap it back. *(Matthew 7:1-2, Galatians 6:7)*

d. Judgements are often made in the foundational years of our lives - in our childhood and may therefore be hidden in our heart and forgotten in our adult life.

e. An expectation follows on from a judgement and this fuels the spiritual dynamic of the judgement. We live out of an inward anticipation of expectant behaviour by which we push people to fulfil our picture of the way things will go. (eg. "Women will always be dominating", "Men can't be trusted")

f. Habits add to the certainty of the judgement becoming a self-fulfilling prophecy.

Notes:

Testimonies For Forgiveness

TESTIMONY I

I was struggling with unforgiveness. I found it hard to forgive my father who was an alcoholic, and was also wayward in his behaviour. My most precious and valuable moments were during the ministry time, when I was able to first pour all my heart out and be set free from the bondage of unforgiveness, rejection and abuse. I also felt the Love of Father God becoming real to me, and sensed the deep touch of my Father's unconditional love.

TESTIMONY II

Growing up, I harboured unforgiveness towards few of my relatives, and over the last year, I had also begun to develop a hatred towards my brother and sister-in-law, since I felt they were very selfish. But, as the session on bitterness and trauma was taught at the 'Healing and Deliverance Conference' I was able to identify my problem. And during my ministry time, as I shared everything with the ministry team member, God helped me to get rid of all my fears and the unforgiveness I was holding onto. I praise God for this, and I hope and pray that this ministry will spread all over India, so that everyone will be blessed.

TESTIMONY III

During the 'Healing and Deliverance Conference', I realized that my condition was like a clogged stream - clogged due to the waste and debris I had dumped in it. I had been trying to remove them over time, but realized that it was beyond me. Recognizing and confessing, "Lord, I need help", began to set things in motion. God revealed that I was harbouring bitterness and unforgiveness towards Him due to the fact that I felt that for 10 years He had not answered my prayers. And though He had revealed this to me, I kept running away from Him every time He called me to talk about my disappointments, and never allowed Him to heal me and restore me. And during this waiting process I decided to take matters into my own hands, and in open rebellion ended up indulging in sin...which explains the truckload of waste that was dumped into my stream. Even though I had told the Lord that I was sorry for the sin I had committed, deep down I felt I was justified in saying that since God hadn't fulfilled my need, I had gone ahead and fulfilled it for myself. Another area that was revealed to me at the 'Healing and Deliverance Conference' was to search my motive for wanting to belong to God's fold. I came to understand that if my decision to belong to God was only to get my needs fulfilled, and not because of Who He is, then I would be disappointed if I felt another prayer was unanswered. Even as I've understood this, I am praying these days that my motives would be to belong to God for Who He is and for what He has already accomplished for me on the cross, and that I would love Him out of this relationship rather than for what I could get out of Him.

Today, I am restored back to my first love. The Healing and Deliverance Conference helped clean my stream.

TESTIMONY IV

For me, forgiving people never came easily. I would smile through everything without letting people know how I really felt. All my emotions were bottled up within me and I'd refuse to deal with it. Coming here changed so much for me. I realized I had an enormous list of people to forgive. My personal ministry helped me to slowly release all these people, and I've never felt lighter before!

Dealing With Emotional Pain

Trying to remain Godly in attitude and behaviour, is a challenge that those seeking God's healing will have to be aware of. The healing process may take time, and keeping the right response is necessary to remain open to God's healing. *(Matthew 19:17)*

6.1 What is Emotional Pain

a. Emotional pain is as real as physical pain. *(Psalm 38:6-8)*
b. It is the opposite of "shalom".

6.2 Where does it come from?

a. Hurtful relationships - short or long term.
b. Acute situations of wounding.
c. Chronic situations of distress.

6.3 Responsibility of the person in emotional pain

a. To dare to be real and acknowledge the pain.
b. To be willing to change their old habits and beliefs. *(Isaiah 53:2, Luke 4:18-19)*

Notes:

6.4 Dangers for those in emotional pain

a. It is very easy to believe the lies of Satan.
b. It is easy to slip into sinful behaviours, to try to dull the pain and meet needs.
c. It is tempting to use unreality and denial to try to negate the pain.
d. Emotional dependence on others is a real problem, especially in a counselling situation.

6.5 Needs of those in emotional pain

a. Unconditional love, caring discipline and clear boundaries.
b. Encouragement.
c. To be treated with dignity.

6.6 Practical ways to survive emotional pain

a. Recognise the need for company, even if withdrawing has been a past habit.
b. Allow yourself to emote at a convenient time, and try not to add more pain to the deep well of buried pain.
c. Work at finding or expanding your creativity.
d. Find things that you enjoy doing, have some fun and laugh :)
e. Allow God's Love to minister to you; and be kind to yourself.
f. Recognise that a little "switching-off" time may be helpful.

Notes:

Testimonies For Emotional Pain

TESTIMONY I

As a young child, I was abused. I'd always felt rejected by my family, but this incident further added to it. I became quiet and reserved and I was very cautious while around people. When I heard about the Encounter with God, I didn't take any real interest. I only went since everyone else was going. I sat through most of the sessions wondering what I was doing there… until they started talking about 'Rejection'. Everything within me wanted to scream! The session on 'Emotional Healing' literally 'opened the flood gates!' I'd never cried the way I did then. I wept and the ministry team person praying for me also wept. It touched me so much, to know that there could be someone who understood my pain. The person hugged me tight and held me close. I felt like a child again, broken on the inside, but as I cried, I felt relief… and lightness. The person still held me tight and I could feel God's Love surround me. I felt special…. accepted. That moment was indescribable. I've loved every bit of the Encounter, and I'm glad I decided to attend this weekend that has made such a huge difference in my life.

TESTIMONY II

I was in a phase of complete spiritual and emotional death. There was no life in me; only pain, regret, guilt and shame. I had cheated on the girl I had promised to marry, and she was devastated when I left her for a Hindu girl, with whom I had a sexual relationship which resulted in a pregnancy and subsequent abortion. Eventually, I had to leave her too since I realized it was an ungodly relationship.

But, I couldn't live with the guilt of breaking their hearts. Every moment all I could hear was them crying and begging me not to leave them. I couldn't live with the guilt, the pain, the regret; if I closed my eyes I would see them crying. I gave up on life, and would weep every night for months on end.

During the session on 'Emotional Healing', I was able to finally forgive myself and let go of all the guilt, regret and shame. I became a new person with a new shot at life; from death to life.

TESTIMONY III

My father passed away when I was 8 years old, and I realised that from then on I had taken on many responsibilities even as a child. This continued through the years. And although I believed that I trusted the Lord, in reality, it was not so. Even serving the Lord felt like a burden to me. But, today I have repented and have decided to walk in the Spirit.

In the past, I also used to find it difficult to relate to others since I had hardened my emotions; to the extent that I found it difficult to show love to my husband and children. But the Lord has healed me even in this area of my life.

TESTIMONY IV

Before coming to this Healing and Deliverance Conference, I remember telling my husband that what I was attending better be a good thing...and now I can assure my husband and the Adonai Ministries that this was not just good, but is one of the best gifts that the Lord has given me in my life!

Here's a little bit about my life –
- -My life was filled with rejection from my parents; they always called me an expensive child - they said they had spent on my education, my growing up, my wedding...and all this was eating me up on the inside. And growing up, since I was the eldest child, I had those responsibilities also on my shoulders.

- -I was sexually abused and in time got hooked to porn sites.

- -Though my family comes from a traditional Christian background, we practiced idolatry and witchcraft.

- -Six months after my wedding, I got pregnant. But since I was consumed with the responsibilities of my family, I resented getting pregnant and did not want the child. But as 5 weeks passed, I tried to make myself understand that this was God's Gift and I had to accept it. In the 6th week of my pregnancy I went to the doctor and was informed that I was suffering from hypothyroidism; being from the medical field I knew that this was a lifelong disease, that I would never be normal again. In my 7th week, I was advised to take a sonography; but before I could, I started bleeding. So, I immediately went for the sonography where they declared that I was carrying a dead child who had no heartbeat.

I lost it completely. I rejected myself and thought that God hated me. I cursed myself and my God! Though my family stood next to me, I felt I had no one. I was lost! When I came to the Healing and Deliverance Conference, God not only revealed the curses that were operating in my life along with the causes of the rejection and fear I faced, but He also faithfully brought me out of it and built up my confidence - that I can be a mother again. I don't have any fear of my sickness or of anything in that matter. All I can say is God gave me a chance to live again. I am born again. I praise God for each day He gives me. I love Him more than anybody in this World.

I once again thank the Adonai team for the blessings they have poured on my family and myself through Christ alone.

TESTIMONY V

I will always remember the Adonai Dehradun Healing and Deliverance Conference as the days of my renewal and restoration. I have been a Christian for a long time and have had a personal relationship with God, but I never realized that the devil had some legal rights in my life and was holding me in bondage over the many areas of my life where I was struggling.

For the first time, I was able to grieve for my dad; not with tears of bitterness, but with the pain a child felt when they lost a father. I was able to forgive my dad from my heart, and as I released him it brought closure and peace in my heart. As I looked into my life, I see what a mess it has been, but what has healed me of a lot of pain is the realization that God has been holding on to me no matter what. To be able to speak out my story without lying and feeling judged, to acknowledge my past and make peace with it, to cry tears of release - all of this has brought me profound joy and happiness. Today, I look at myself and love the person I am. I look at others and love them also. I laugh out loud and smile with all my heart. I enjoy what I see. I am glad and happy that God loves me more than what I know or understand.

I had come even last year for the Healing and Deliverance Conference, but was so overwhelmed with thoughts about my father and the inner damage he had caused - he had caused my family and myself immense fear and trauma in many areas of our lives. He was an angry man who had all the vices in this world, and that also resulted in him having a daughter through an illicit relationship. So, the last time I had focused on receiving healing in these areas.

During this Healing and Deliverance Conference, as the teaching was going on, I realized that I had not dealt with many other areas of my life in the previous year. I hadn't dealt with the areas like generational iniquity, trauma from childhood due to abuse, astrology, horoscope, agreements made with the Catholic Church at the time of marriage, etc. I was keen to deal with them this time, so that I would be free from the demonic hold of the enemy.

Praise God, today I am free. I now eagerly look forward to the Prayer Ministry Seminar, so that I can be trained, since it is my desire to be of help to those who are still suffering and need to be free.

Relationships And Soul Ties

7.1 Introduction

a. Our whole life is centered on relationships. God Himself is a Relational Being; God said, *"Let Us make man in Our image, according to Our likeness..." (Genesis 1:26)*

b. God created us as relational beings and intended for us to relate to each other. *(Genesis 2:18)*

c. The ability to form relationships is God given; sin stepped in and distorted it. *(I John 1:7)*

d. There are different levels of relationships; from the closeness and intimacy of a husband and wife to the casual relationship of an acquaintance. The quality of our life is affected by the well being of these relationships, especially with those who are closest to us.

e. Our highest and lowest experiences of life revolve around relationships. For example:
   i. Friendships
   ii. Marriage
   iii. Having a baby
   iv. Death

f. Love has meaning only when it is in relationships.

g. The Fall *(Genesis 3)* and its consequences had an immediate effect on the quality of Adam and Eve's relationships.

Notes:

h. God meant relationships to be a blessing, but it resulted in harm because of sin. The same is true for us today.

7.2 Four important aspects of wholesome relationships

There are four important aspects which dictate the depth and quality of our relationships. These are **Respect, Understanding, Trust** and **Agape Love.** For these to be meaningful they need to be mutual.

a. Respect, Honour - *Romans 12:10*
b. Understanding - *Romans 12:9-21, 15:1-5*
   We need to be in relationships where we feel others understand us to a certain degree. When someone is not prepared to understand us or listen to us, we feel disregarded, put down, perhaps isolated.
c. Trust - *Ephesians 5:21, James 5:16, Zechariah 8:16*
   There are various levels of trust eg. work, society, church, family, marital etc.
d. Agape Love - *John 14:34, 15:12-17, I Corinthians 13*
   This unconditional love should be the strongest in marriage, and in families. A love which is there even when there is failure and disappointment.

These four aspects of **Respect, Understanding, Trust** and **Agape Love** will vary in different kinds of relationships (work, social, Church, family).

7.3 Failure and unwholesome relationships

- Because none of us are perfect, we all sin. There will be breakdown in even the closest and lasting relationships. The enemy of our souls, Satan, will seek to disrupt our relationships.
- Where there is fear, control, abuse, manipulation, deceit, unfaithfulness, violence, etc., it will have a profound effect on us.

7.4 Relationships and Soul Ties

A relationship is the mutual sharing of life between two or more people. Relationships are not merely physical, but they are also spiritual. The spiritual element in a relationship is called a 'soul tie'.

Notes:

We must realize that as we walk this earth there is a spiritual issue behind all of man's relationships and activities. *(Psalm 133, Matthew 18:18)*

The Bible uses many other terms to describe this spiritual tie or what we call a 'soul tie'. The following terms are used to describe the depth and effect these soul ties have on human relationships.

a. Yoke

The word describing the linking of two animals is used of human relationships. This may be restrictive or it may be good for discipline, training and guidance.

- Jacob and Esau *(Genesis 27:40)* where there was deceit and hatred.
- Christians and Non-Christians. *(II Corinthians 6:14)*
- Jesus and ourselves. *(Matthew 11:29-30)*

b. Bondage

Relationships where there is loss of freedom:

- A religious bondage. *(Galatians 5:1)*
- Children of Israel in slavery. *(Ezekiel 2:23)*
- The word 'bond' is linked to covenant relationships *(Ezekiel 20:37)* - so, some bonds can be good.

c. Knitting

An intertwining, tying together:

- David and Jonathan's souls were knit together. *(I Samuel 18:1)*
- We are 'knit together bones and sinews', in the womb. *(Job 10:11)*
- The Church, knit together in love *(Colossians 2:2)* - and as the body (Church) is knit together, it grows. *(Ephesians 4:16)*

d. Joined

Cleave (AV), cling to, stick to. In the OT it is mentioned 52 times including in our relationship to God, and in the NT it means to be glued to.

- Husband to cleave to his wife, 'one flesh'. *(Genesis 2:24)*
- Note that God is involved in this gluing *(Matthew 19:5-6)* - linked with sexual intercourse.
- Applies to ungodly sex. *(I Corinthians 6:17)*

Notes:

e. **Bound Up**

A spiritual tying together:
- The lives of Jacob and Benjamin were tied together *(Genesis 44:22,30)* out of fear!

These words and terms express the reality of relationships - ties which have a great influence on our lives. We are not islands to ourselves, but live affecting others and being affected by others.

7.5 How are they Formed?

a. <u>Through birth, not choice</u>
- Generational
- Siblings
- Relatives

b. <u>Through exercise of our choice</u>
- Friendships, marriage, sexual relations.
- Groups, work, organisations, where there is an allegiance.
- Religious groups, new age, where there is a spiritual element.

c. <u>Abuse</u>
- Abuse, violence, trauma.
- Under the control and domination of someone.

d. <u>Through force</u> - violence | domination.

7.6 Relationship Ties and Bonds can be a Blessing or a Curse

In a good relationship the spiritual covering is Godly. There is freedom, there is edification and every blessing that God intended to be. In an ungodly relationship the spiritual hold is not of God. It is under a spiritual covering of darkness. *(Ephesians 2:2)*

Relationships are an integral part of what we do in this world. So, when we sin, we enter a place of bondage instead of a place of freedom. When we look at relationships and soul ties, we need to ask our self, "What is the spiritual hold over this relationship?"

Notes:

7.7 Relationship Ties and Bonds can be a Blessing or a Curse

A good soul tie is a good spiritual union between two people. Jesus wants us to be bound together with the bond of love. "… You shall Love your neighbor as yourself" *(Matthew 22:39)*
The bond of unity that God wants us to have in the Body of Christ is Love. The opposite of love is fear.
Examples:
- Paul and Timothy *(I Corinthians 4:17)*
- Ruth and Naomi *(Ruth 1:16-17)*

7.8 What are Ungodly Ties?

Ungodly soul ties are always about control in its various forms, including an individual allowing another to control him/her. If relationships are about yielding, then the enemy wants to pervert it and turn it into control, and that becomes an ungodly soul tie.

a. Ways of control:
- Emotional blackmail
- Anger
- Love
- Fear

b. The consequences of ungodly soul ties are:
- Physical sickness in people's bodies.
- Damage to the will (just like a wrongful yoke on the back of those animals).

c. There is no control between adults in the Kingdom of God. There is a rightful order.
Jesus never controlled His disciples. An ungodly soul tie can cause one to be damaged in their spirit by relationships that God never intended us to experience. *(Luke 13:10)*

Examples:
- Rape, abuse, guilt, intimidation
- Parents *(Genesis 44:30)*
- Vows and agreements
- Organisational

Notes:

7.9 Our Free-Will - the Ordinance of God

All relationships must depend on free-will choice. We need Godly authority.
(Deuteronomy 30:19-20)

7.10 Boundaries

(Proverbs 4:23)

Notes:

Testimonies For Relationships And Soul Ties

TESTIMONY I

I watched my parents in the act of having sex when I was just a child. The memory of that night remained with me for years. Soon, sexual perversion sank in. I would have sex with prostitutes, watch lots of pornography and hang out with the wrong crowd.

Some time ago, I was abused by these 'friends' of mine, and this completely shattered me. I didn't understand what was happening, and didn't realise that it would affect me in such a huge way. I was confused about my sexuality, and suddenly everything felt wrong. I knew I needed answers.

I had attended the Encounter the previous year. I was in desperate need of answers and I knew I had hit rock bottom. The sessions were very new to me, and I hadn't expected them to be so apt. I couldn't wait for personal ministry since I had so much to unburden. I was prayed for, and I thought I'd been healed of the guilt, the shame and all those perverse thoughts that were always lurking around in my head. I went back and I expected to feel clean and new... but, things just went back to the way they were. I barely lasted a day! The feeling of hopelessness came rushing back all over again... and this time in double measure!

I didn't think anything would change at this Encounter either. But God's timing is perfect! The topics taught were exactly the same as the last time when I had attended, but this time everything seemed so much clearer. I could relate to everything, especially the teaching on 'Sexual Bondage'. During my time of personal ministry as I was being prayed for, I closed my eyes trying to push those thoughts that were distracting me, and tried to concentrate. Suddenly, I saw myself surrounded by blazing flames, and dancing around them were the ugliest demons I'd ever seen. They seemed to be celebrating over something... over me! The noise was deafening. I wanted to shut it all out, when suddenly a beam of white light pierced through the flames! And as the light grew brighter, the demons fled and the noise lessened. The place was flooded with the light, and now I could see angels dancing around me, singing and rejoicing!

I opened my eyes and realized that my battle had been won; I came out victorious. It was such a liberating feeling - something I'll never forget. The King of the Universe is indeed my King too! I am completely free now. Thank you for this wonderful experience!

TESTIMONY II

I was born in a Christian family and would attend church regularly, following all the rituals. In 1990 I accepted the Lord Jesus. But along the way I fell from grace and got hooked into sexual immorality and other issues like anger, controlling others, trying to prove myself all the time, rejection and unforgiveness. Today, I have been cleansed, healed and delivered at this Healing and Deliverance Conference, and I am experiencing His unconditional love and goodness. Thank you Adonai Ministries for your help and encouragement in bringing me back to the Lord Jesus' fold once again.

LEARNINGS –
-Many times we cope with problems, but I've now learnt that God doesn't want us to keep coping with the issues; rather, God wants to heal us and lead us to a victorious life.
-Healing comes when our attitude is changed from anger and hatred, to forgiveness.
-Our behaviour cannot change if our belief is not right.

TESTIMONY III

I had a load of sin. Lust was rampant. So was drinking and sexual encounters with men. For 30 years, I lived with these bondages. But after my ministry, I feel like I had a good scrub and a scented bath, from the inside. The hollowness I once felt is no longer there. I know that God loves me, that Jesus saved me, and that His Holy Spirit now lives on the inside of me. I feel so happy; it's great to be free!

TESTIMONY IV

Before I came to the Healing and Deliverance Conference, I was bound by things that had happened in my past; I was broken in spirit and depressed, having faced rejection, abuse, etc. On the first day, I was in bed because I was suffering from spondylitis. On the second day, during the time of worship, God healed me from the pain and I felt His Love filling me.

I had lacked a relationship with God though I longed for it. I was only 13 years old when I got hooked on to porn, and because of that, I got into masturbation. But after my personal time of ministry, God set me free, and I no longer feel the urge to masturbate or watch porn.

I also Praise God that during the 'Holy Spirit' session, I received the gift of tongues. This has been the best week of my life. I thank God and Adonai for all that He has done in my life.

TESTIMONY V

The Healing and Deliverance Conference will always have a special place in my heart; this was where I rediscovered my passion for Christ, experienced His Presence, and was delivered from my iniquities and struggles.

I had a difficult childhood. I grew up feeling rejected and lonely, and along the way was sexually abused by 2 men, one of whom was a relative. This messed up my understanding about my sexuality. In time, I also ended up sexually abusing a few of my younger cousins, both male and female.

To satisfy the vacuum within me I resorted to pornography, masturbation, smoking and drinking.

I remained distant from my family since I didn't feel loved by them; I was constantly yelled at and beaten at home. Things between my parents were not good. My dad would beat my mum, and my mum always suspected him of having affairs with other women. This she eventually found was true in 2004, just before my dad passed away due to cancer; he himself confessed his past misdeeds on his death bed. Witnessing this made me feel sorry for my mum, and I ended up becoming very sensitive to women and children who were abused. Even reading newspapers articles where crimes were committed against women and children would anger me.

In 2004 I was baptised; this was a couple of months before my dad passed away. But after his death, I became angry with God for not saving my dad, despite my hatred towards him.

As life went on, bad company was my constant companion, both in college and university abroad. To satisfy my sexual pleasures, I had sexual relations with 20 - 25 women, many of whom were call girls.

My fear of God was situation based and momentary; I sought His help when I needed a job, or wanted to get out of some self-inflicted trouble (something I was really good at finding myself in). Though I have attended other deliverance meetings a couple of years ago, I still suffered with a sense of insecurity, anger, pain, loneliness and rejection. Coming back to India, porn and masturbation were temporary pleasures, though I would feel guilty later. And this vicious cycle continued. At the same time, I was also very active with my Church, taught in Sunday School, and was popular among the Church youth.

But, after attending the Healing and Deliverance Conference, I have only God to thank; He ministered to me and delivered me from my problems and bondages. Thank You, Jesus!

TESTIMONY VI

I Praise God for choosing me. I thank God for making me more than a conqueror in Christ Jesus. I love You, Lord. As I again put it... "I am blessed and totally free". May the Lord give Adonai Ministries more grace to minister to more of His children and set them free.

I have learned a lot and I believe that He has a great purpose for my life. Born on this earth, 40 years ago and born again for the last 22 years, I never knew I was carrying such baggage in my life. I remember my parents telling me that I was dedicated to a bishop, but never thought that it would be one of my problems. I always thought it to be pride. But on the day when my ministry time took place, I found myself being delivered from the spirit of religiosity.

I attended this Healing and Deliverance Conference with the desire to get rid of the baggage of my past, but I didn't realise that I was carrying a much heavier load than I realised. I was abused when I was in the 3rd std and that resulted in me being bound by the spirit of lust. I never knew that I had in fact turned into an abuser - an abuser of my own body and others. During ministry, the team prayed for me and I felt God setting me free, and at that moment I knew I was delivered.

Today, I am free and am determined to walk with Christ even after I leave this Conference. I know that I can do all things through Christ Jesus who strengthens me.

CHAPTER 8

Overcoming Fear

What is Fear?

Fear is a God given emotion that motivates us. God intended that the emotion of fear would be a protector, warning us of danger, and so that would motivate us to do something to protect ourselves. If it is a protector, it is good, because it exists to protect us.

Fear can also be a master; when fear becomes our master it then controls and keeps us in torment.

8.1 Two Types of Fear

a. <u>Fear of God</u>
   i. This is an expression in the OT meaning 'reverential trust', including the hatred of evil.
   ii. To fear the Lord is to hate evil.
   iii. Jesus delighted in the fear of the Lord. *(Isaiah 11:1-3)*
   iv. Fearing the Lord is about submitting to His Infinite Power and Authority.
   v. *Proverbs 22:4*
      "Humility and the fear of the LORD bring wealth and honor and life."
   vi. Jesus also encouraged us to only fear God and not the enemy or his works. *(Matthew 10:26-28)*

Notes:

b. <u>Ungodly Fear (fear from satan)</u>
   The word fear is first mentioned in *Genesis 3:10*.
   i. Fear entered when man tried to hide and find his own covering.
   ii. Fear comes into our lives when we are outside God's covering, through circumstances, ignorance or disobedience.
   iii. Fear is a destiny stealer.
   iv. The Kingdom of God has no place for ungodly fear.
   In *(Matthew 6)*, Jesus is challenging us on this whole issue of being fearful and anxious. There are 365 verses in the Bible that say do not fear.

Fear Is Not A Thing, But A Person

Medical doctors say that fear and anxiety are the root causes of many physical disorders and sicknesses. Very often, it is not the disease that kills us, but fear.

Fear Is The Opposite Of Faith
What Faith Is To God, Fear Is To The Enemy

Other words for fear are:

- Anxiety - *(Matthew 6:25-34)*
- Worry - *(I Peter 5:7-8)*
- Terror
- Timidity - *(II Timothy 1:7)*
- Panic - *(Deuteronomy 20:1-4)*
- Phobias
- Dread

8.2 Common Phobias

i. Fear of being outside the house
ii. Claustrophobia

Notes:

iii. Social phobia

iv. Fear of death

v. Fear of being alone

vi. Fear of thunder

vii. Fear of insects, birds, spiders - *(Genesis 9:2)*

viii. Fear of illnesses or injections, doctors, dentists, blood, hospitals

ix. Fear of the dark

8.3 The Effects of Fear

a. <u>Body, soul and spirit</u>
- Bodily manifestation of fear include trembling, shaking, heart racing, breathlessness, sweating, etc.. *(I Kings 1:3-4, Daniel 5:6)*
- Soul manifestation of fear concerns the mind and emotions, trauma, crying, panicky, fear, negative emotions. *(Matthew 11:29)*
- Spirit - unbelief produces fear, and lies can become a progressive cycle experienced in the spirit.
- *(II Timothy 1:7)*. This leads to the conclusion, for example, "God does not love me enough to rescue me from this fearful situation". This fear is bigger than God.

b. <u>The Role of the Demonic</u>
- The Godly purpose of fear is so that we are warned of danger and run into the Arms of God. When we store ungodly fear in us, it then gives the enemy authority to act.
- Through trauma, sin, and believing lies, we become uncovered and give place for fear to enter. Spirits of fear can take a hold and bring us into deep bondage.
- Occult involvement.
- If we are frequently threatened about our well-being, then we may get into a state of being constantly fearful - 'jumpy'.
- Generalized anxiety - being fearful of everything and everyone.
- Panic attacks.
- Fear of rejection and the fear of failure.

Notes:

8.4 Identification of Fears

a. Is the root of my fear based in unbelief or lack of faith to trust God?
b. Where did it come in? (Generational, occult involvement, trauma)
c. Ask God to link the memory to the emotion.

8.5 How to Overcome our Fears?

a. The Perfect Love of Jesus casts out all fear.
    I John 4:18
    "There is no fear in love. But perfect love drives out fear, because fear has to do with punishment. The one who fears is not made perfect in love."

b. Lordship of Jesus over every area of our lives.
c. Deliverance from spirits of fear and unbelief.
d. Renounce the lies that you have believed and apply the truth.
e. *I Peter 5:7*
    "Cast all your anxiety on Him because He cares for you."

The Only Power Satan Has Is The Power Of The Lie

Notes:

CHAPTER 9

Belief Systems

9.1 What we think and what we believe affects our emotional, relational and spiritual development and behaviour

Proverbs 23:7 (NKJV)
"For as he thinks in his heart, so is he."

9.2 Belief systems and mind-sets

a. The way we think, or what we believe, develops from a very early age, becoming our belief systems, which are deeply rooted in our inner being.

b. These beliefs can be social, political, and religious. They can either be good, bad or a mixture of both.

c. A mind-set is a pattern of thinking which is so entrenched in us, that our thoughts and consequent behaviours come out of that particular pattern in the same way every time. *(II Corinthians 10:5)*

d. All faulty belief systems need to be brought to the light *(I John 1:7)*. They are, however, often deeply rooted and unknown to ourselves, and are our 'blind spots'. *(Matthew 7:3)*

Notes:

9.3 There are beliefs in the 'mind' and there are beliefs in our 'spirit', and these two beliefs can be very conflicting

a. In our minds we know it is true, but in our spirit we don't feel it is true.
b. Our spirit, which is the very core of our being, includes our beliefs, our identity and our sexuality. *(Romans 10:9-11)*

9.4 Why is it important to deal with core lies?

We are a product of what we believe. *(Hebrews 11:6, 10:35)*

9.5 Three things that the enemy will NOT want us to believe

a. The Truth about God.
b. The truth about ourselves.
c. The truth about others.

❖ **Satan, the father of lies** *(John 8:44-45)*
- The only weapon satan has, is the power of lies or deception.
- Each one of us have built our lives on certain beliefs regarding who God is, what we believe about ourselves, and what we believe about others, based on the positive or negative circumstances of life.

  For Example:

  "If I live a good life and do good to others, that is sufficient."

  "If you have money you will have everything."

9.6 Where does the lie come from?

a. Our wounding - If a person was abandoned by their parents, then abandonment becomes a belief.
b. Wrong information - Religious beliefs, superstitions.
c. Wrong perceptions - "Everyone hates me".
d. Absence of affirmation - always been criticized.
e. Bad and traumatic experiences - the child believes that it was his/her fault that parents got divorced.
f. The Enemy.

Notes:

When we receive lies in our spirit as truth and act upon them as truth, it establishes that lie as a core belief.

9.7 How do we get rid of the lies in our core belief? *Mark 9:21*

John 8:30

"Jesus said, 'If you hold to my teaching, you are really my disciples. (32) Then you will know the truth, and the truth will set you free'."

Notes:

Testimonies For Belief Systems

TESTIMONY I

I came with a lot of pain and unrest. During worship, I started crying and did not understand why I couldn't stop. But, I also experienced much relief after each session, even as I began to understand the Word of God from a different perspective. God spoke to me about the strongholds of fear, guilt, vows, superstitions, belief systems and unforgiveness that I had carried. He also delivered me from the idolatry that I had practiced in the past.

I suffered from arthritis, and even in this God was so Faithful. He brought to light the lie that I had believed - I had all along believed that God could heal me, but didn't want to heal me. Today, I believe that God wants to heal me and wants me to be joyful.

TESTIMONY II

Earlier this year, I got married, but was not able to conceive. In my heart, I had a lot of fear regarding having a baby. Looking at my past, my parents fought all the time, and looking at my present, I had a mother-in-law who was very controlling; she controlled my husband and caused a lot of trouble. Hence, I found myself unable to pray and ask God for a child, fearing that I wouldn't be able to provide for the baby, or take care of the child. Another thought that worried me was of my mother-in-law would reject the baby if I had a daughter, and if I had a son, I feared she would take him away from me.

So, during my time of personal ministry, one of the ministry team members prayed that God would bless me with a child in His time. As they finished praying, the cards came back from the intercession room, and one of them had an image of me looking very happy and carrying a baby in my arms! I now have the assurance that when God blesses me with a child I will be very happy. There will be no fear.

Today, I am walking out of this place with God's promise, and in God's freedom. Nowadays, I wake up every morning with a song of praise to Him.

Thank you for helping me go back to my first love - Jesus. I came here feeling so far away from the Lord, but I am going back as a daughter of God, knowing the Father's Love for me, and loving Him more than ever before.

CHAPTER 10

Spiritual Realms

An understanding from the Scriptures of the Heavenly Realms is a necessary foundation to the Deliverance Ministry.

There is a Spiritual Kingdom that submits to the Will of God, and a Kingdom of darkness that opposes His Will. (Matthew 11:12)

These kingdoms are not in any way equal and opposite, but there is a spiritual battle taking place between them, which affects every Christian.

10.1 God - Father, Son and Holy Spirit

a. God, the Creator, has sovereign power and authority over the created realms - the Heavenly and the Earthly realms. *(Psalm 103:19, Colossians 1:16)*
b. Jesus is equal with God the Father. *(Philippians 2:6)*
c. The Holy Spirit is "another of the same type" as Jesus. *(John 14:16)*

10.2 The Heavenly Realm in Obedience to God

a. <u>Angels seem to have different rankings and significance, example -</u>
   - Archangel - Michael *(Jude 9, Daniel 10:13&21)*

Notes:

- Chief Angel - Gabriel *(Daniel 8:16, 9:21, Luke 1:19, 26)*
- Cherubim - *(Genesis 3:24, Ezekiel 10:1,20-22, Revelation 4:6-9)*
- Seraphim - *(Isaiah 6:1-8)*
- Angels - *(Revelation 5:11, 7:1, 8:6, 10:1, 15:1)*

b. <u>God has given the Angels certain jobs and functions:</u>
- To be in God's presence. *(Matthew 18:10)*
- Worshipping God and the Son of God. *(Hebrews 1:6)*
- Rejoicing in His works. *(Job 38:7)*
- Executing God's Will. *(Psalm 103:20-21)*
- Assisting and protecting believers. *(Hebrews 1:14, I Kings 19:5, Matthew 4:11)*
- Affecting the affairs of Nations. *(Daniel 10:12-13, 21, 11:1, 12:1)*
- Watching over the interests of Churches. *(I Timothy 5:21, Revelation 2-3)*
- Releasing punishment on His enemies. *(Acts 12:23, II Samuel 24:16)*
- Extraordinary acts. *(Acts 12:6-7)*
- Teaching the law. *(Acts 7:53, Galatians 3:19, Hebrews 2:2)*
- Messengers from God. *(Luke 1:19, 26)*

10.3 The Heavenly Realm in Rebellion Against God

a. Lucifer - the anointed cherub. *(Ezekiel 28:14)*
b. The fall of Lucifer. *(Isaiah 14:12-15)*

c. <u>The names of satan indicate his works and nature:</u>
- Satan the adversary of God and believers. *(I Chronicles 21:1, Matthew 4:10, Zechariah 3:1, I Peter 5:8)*
- Accuser of the brethren. *(Revelation 12:10)*
- Apollyon, the destroyer. *(John 10:10, Revelation 9:11)*
- Liar and murderer. *(John 8:44)*
- Devourer - *(I Peter 5:8-9)*
- Deceiver - *(Revelation 12:9, II Corinthians 11:3, 14)*
- Serpent, dragon. *(Revelation 12:3-9)*
- Beelzebub - Philistine god of the flies - the name used by Jews to denote the devil. *(Matthew 12:24)*

Notes:

- Tempter -*(Matthew 4:3)*
- Thief - *(John 10:10)*

d. Satan is limited in location, knowledge, time and power. *(Job 1:6-12, Acts 19:15)*

e. Demons are agents of satan.
<u>They can also be called unclean spirits. Demons have the following characteristics:</u>
- Serve satan. *(Matthew 12:24)*
- Are living; can hear and respond. *(Luke 4:34 -35, Mark 3:11-12)*
- Have intelligence and knowledge. *(Mark 1:23-24)*
- Have emotions. *(Matthew 8:29-31, James 2:19)*
- Have spiritual substance, and seek a body to act through. *(Luke 10:19, 8:33, Revelation 16:13)*
- Have a will. *(Matthew 12:43-44, Luke 11:24-26, Mark 5:11-13)*
- Drive and torment people. *(Mark 5:5)*
- Give supernatural strength. *(Luke 8:29)*
- Have specific job functions - to bring infirmity *(Luke 13:11)* and slavery to fear *(Romans 8:15)*, promote lying *(II Chronicles 18:22)* jealousy *(Numbers 5:14)* and deception *(I Timothy 4:1)*.
- Can work in groups, under an authority structure. *(Luke 8:2, Ephesians 6:12)*
- Are legalistic, and know where they have rights. *(Acts 19:15, Ephesians 4:27)*
- Recognise the Authority of Jesus and know their end. *(Matthew 25:41, Matthew 8:29)*
- Do not die when humans die.

f. <u>Possible effects of demonization; the "fruit" of unclean spirits:</u>
- Torment
- Driven-ness, sometimes through an inner voice
- Inability to change to Godly ways
- Death wishes and suicidal tendencies
- Compulsions, despising, overwhelming emotional disturbance, antisocial behaviour
- Disease
- Irrational fears
- Occult attraction and power

Notes:

g. The inevitable end for satan and his demons is the lake of fire.
    (Revelation 20:7-15, Matthew 25:41-46)

10.4 The structure of the kingdom of darkness

a. There are rulers and authorities in the Heavenly places hostile to God and mankind. *(Colossians 2:14-15)*
b. This kingdom of darkness has satan as the ruler. *(Ephesians 2:2, Matthew 12:24, Acts 26:18)*
c. The desire of this kingdom and its ruler is to separate man from God, in order that man might remain in submission to satan. *(Luke 4:7)*

d. Within the kingdom of darkness, there is a structure of authority beneath satan. *(Ephesians 6:12)*
   - There are principalities (territories ruled by fallen spiritual princes), rulers (the spiritual control behind ungodly authority) and powers (the spiritual promotion of iniquity).
   - There are fallen spiritual princes over Nations. *(Daniel 10:13, 20)*
   - When man is disobedient, he gives the enemy spiritual authority over the ground, organisations or buildings that he occupies. *(Leviticus 18:27)*

e. Some demonic powers desire to express their nature through a human being. *(Mark 5:7-8)*
f. All rulers, authorities and powers, for all time, are under the Feet of Jesus Christ. *(Ephesians 1:20-23)*
g. In Christ, we are encouraged to pull down strongholds *(II Corinthians 10:4)*, silence the enemy *(Psalm 8:2)*, bind the rulers *(Psalm 149:5-9, Matthew 18:18, Mark 3:27)* and cast out demons *(Matthew 10:8)*.

Notes:

CHAPTER 11

Restoring The Human Spirit

11.1 The Functions of the Human Spirit

a. <u>The primary function of the human spirit is to be the life spring of the being</u>
   i.   To receive from God the life for our body and soul. *(James 2:26, Luke 23:46)*
   ii. To communicate and encourage life to others; spirit to spirit.
   iii. To receive "new birth". *(John 3:6)*

b. <u>Ongoing functions of the human spirit includes:</u>
   i.   To bring comfort and strength to our body and soul. *(Psalm 42:5, II Corinthians 7:13)*
   ii. To reveal the things of God. *(Ephesians 1:17)*
   iii. To bring conviction through our conscience. *(Romans 2:15)*
   iv. To release our creativity.
   v.   To enable true Worship of God. *(John 4:23)*
   vi. To empower all of the being. *(Proverbs 18:14)*
   vii. To facilitate the plans of God.

Notes:

11.2 **Healing the human spirit**

a. <u>How is the human spirit fed and restored?</u>

   i. **Love (Nurture)** - There is nothing to compare with God's Plan for each of us, which is to be unconditionally loved and accepted. The value God puts on us is immeasurable.

   ii. **Free will, time, space and safe boundaries** - We all need the freedom to choose, to make mistakes, to learn, to think, to feel, to grow and express ourselves without fear.

   iii. **Relationships** - Our relationship with our Heavenly Father and with others are vital to the building of our human spirits.

   iv. **Anchoring** - Many people with damage in their human spirits sense a feeling of being adrift, unsafe and unanchored, and not a part of God's Family.

b. <u>Practical ways that God designed for us to receive His Life and Health in our human spirit:</u>

   i. Release of our creativity in any form: playing games, crafts, gardening, walking, dance, music, writing, sports, etc...

   ii. 'Being' as opposed to 'doing', and having no pressurised objective.

   iii. **Choosing** - Choosing for myself or choosing something for others, brings satisfaction and value. God likes and enjoys our choices.

   iv. **Having fun** - The release of laughter, humour and play is God given, and releases our pressure and hardships from within.

   v. **Companionship** - Friendship and shared interests are a part of health to our human spirits. Animals also can play a part in comforting us.

   vi. **Working** - Work brings value to us. Being obsessed about work, however, is de-valuing and out of balance with God's intention for us to have re-creation and rest.

c. <u>Spiritual ways for God to bring restoration to the human spirit are:</u>

   i. Meditating and dwelling on God's Word and allowing it to penetrate our inner being (spirit) rather than our mind.

   ii. Prayer and intercession, which will bring God's truth and comfort to the human spirit.

   iii. Listening to edifying praise and worship, or to tapes of well-balanced Bible teaching.

   iv. The 'Rhema' Word.

Notes:

CHAPTER 12

How Demons Gain Access

If the enemy can gain places of authority and power in our lives, we need to know, how? This truth gives us the opportunity for freedom from bondages from the past, and the knowledge of how to keep from defilement in the future.

12.1 The basis for demonic intrusion in man

a. The whole world that is in disobedience to God, lies in the authority and power of the evil one. *(I John 5:19)*

b. Satan exercises power through the demonic realm. *(Matthew 12:24)*

c. Satan's dominion (or realm of authority) is any place of spiritual darkness. *(Acts 26:18)*

d. He seeks to hold us in captivity to his authority through our disobedience to God's Will. *(Ephesians 2:2, II Timothy 2:25-26, Galatians 4:8-10)*

e. When we "participate… with the sons of disobedience… in deeds of darkness" *(Ephesians 5:8-11)* knowingly or unknowingly *(Leviticus 5:17)*, we become "partakers with them… of God's wrath" and of "the spirit that is now working in the sons of disobedience" *(Ephesians 2:2)*.

f. This can lead to the enemy having a 'place' (Greek = topos) of authority in us, even as believers *(Ephesians 4:27)*. We can call this place a 'foothold'. Demonic power may become established to maintain this foothold and promote the disobedience to God's Will. Jesus, being sinless, gave no such foothold. *(John 14:30, II Corinthians 5:21)*

Notes:

12.2 Demonic footholds can be established through our willing participation in sin

a. Idolatry; false religion. *(Exodus 20:1-5, Deuteronomy 18:9, Psalm 115:4-8, I Corinthians 10:14-21)*

b. Occult activity. *(Deuteronomy 18:10-14)*

c. Owning occult objects. *(Joshua 6:18, Deuteronomy 7:25-26)*

d. Submitting to addictions. *(I Corinthians 6:12, Titus 2:3)*

e. <u>Immorality</u>
   - Fornication which includes Premarital Sex or Trial Marriage. *(I Corinthians 5:1, I Corinthians 6:18, I Corinthians 7:2, I Corinthians 10:8, Galatians 5:19, Ephesians 5:3, Colossians 3:5, I Thessalonians 4:3, Jude 1:7, Revelation 2:14, 20-21)*
   - Sex with forbidden relatives (Incest). *(I Corinthians 5:1, Leviticus 18)*
   - Adultery - *(I Corinthians 6:9-20, Matthew 5:27-31)*
   - Oral, anal and other perverted sexual practices. *(Romans 1:24, Genesis 19)*
   - Pornography and fantasy. *(Galatians 5:16-20)*
   - Masturbation/auto sexuality. *(Galatians 5:16-19)*
   - Bestiality - *(Leviticus 18:23)*
   - Homosexuality and lesbianism. *(Romans 1:26-27, Leviticus 18:22)*
   - Transvestism and trans-sexuality. *(Romans 1:27, Genesis 1:27)*
   - Sexual abuse and rape. *(Judges 19:22-29, Leviticus 18:6)*
   - Masochistic and sadistic sex. *(Romans 1:24)*
   - Bondage sex - *(Romans 1:28-29, Galatians 5:24)*
   - Telephone sex/cyber sex.
   - Voyeurism.
   - Continuing in deliberate sin such as lying or stealing.
   - Self rejection and death wish. *(I Corinthians 3:17, Psalm 139:14)*
   - Cursing with words. *(Matthew 5:22, James 3:8-12, Ephesians 4:26)*
   - Unforgiveness - *(Matthew 18:33-34)*
   - Seeking to control. *(I Kings 21:7-8, II Kings 9:22, John 6:66-67)*
   - Violence and murder (including abortion). *(Matthew 5:21, Psalm 139:13, James 2:26)*

Notes:

12.3 Demonic footholds can be established through our unwilling participation in sin through a lack of Godly cover or knowledge

a. Being visited by generational iniquity. *(Nehemiah 1:6-7, Leviticus 26:39-40, Exodus 20:5)*

b. Believing lies about God, ourselves and others. *(II Corinthians 10:4-5, I Timothy 4:1)*

c. Being controlled by others. *(Genesis 27, Matthew 19:5)*

d. Being overwhelmed by fear. *(Romans 8:15, Philippians 4:6-7, Mark 6:50)*

e. <u>Receiving abuse:</u>
   - Physical - *(Proverbs 4:14-17, Psalm 18:48)*
   - Verbal, emotional and mental - *(Psalm 55:21, Proverbs 26:2, Ecclesiastes 10:20)*
   - Sexual and spiritual - *(II Samuel 13:19-20, Matthew 5:28)*

f. Receiving rejection. *(Psalm 27:10)*

g. Submitting to the spiritual powers over defiled land or buildings. *(Leviticus 18:27-28)*

h. Unguarded contact with the dead (including miscarriage). *(Numbers 19:11, Matthew 5:17, Hebrews 2:14)*

i. Vulnerability through infirmity and disorders. *(Luke 17:19, Acts 10:38)*

j. Being overwhelmed by trauma - accidents, emotional overload, loss and bereavement. *(Luke 4:18, Ephesians 5:15-16)*

k. Submitting to healing methods and medicine outside God's covering. *(Jeremiah 17:13-14, Matthew 12:24)*

l. Most of the above can give opportunity for establishing ungodly soul ties, which are themselves an opening for a demonic foothold. *(Proverbs 5:22, II Corinthians 6:14-17)*

12.4 Demonic footholds can be established through our willing participation in sin

a. It is God who reveals any places of darkness within us if we ask Him. *(Psalm 139:23-24, Luke 11:34-36, Proverbs 20:27)*

b. Our human spirit knows our spiritual condition. *(John 13:21, I Corinthians 2:11)*

Notes:

Testimonies For How Demons Gain Access

TESTIMONY I

Rejection was a major issue in my life. Even though my parents brought me up giving me all I needed, I always felt that there was something missing. I remember always craving for my mom to give me a warm hug. But I never got it, and never expressed this desire to my mom. Apart from this, there was also generational rejection that was coming down our family line. So, due to the rejection I faced, I made an imaginary friend for myself, someone in whom I could find a companion. After my 10th std we moved cities, and I now had my own room, which became a place of solace for me; I would always run to my room for comfort. My room faced a church which also had a cemetery, and I used to keep looking there, for hours, trying to see if ghosts existed. Though this initially was fun, I slowly started getting obsessed with the unknown, and had all weird thoughts about the same. In time, I began asking the spirits to come and carry me out of my home to a nicer place.

It was at the *Healing and Deliverance Conference* that I realized that all of this was rooted in rejection, and it was only as I dealt with it that I realized the magnitude of the mess I was in. Though the spirit of rejection and the imaginary friend were cast out, I couldn't let go of the bond I had with my room. But, once the ministry team member dealt with it, I experienced freedom.

There was also another area that I was set free from. Being the firstborn, my dad loved me a lot, but he also expected me to be the boy of the house. This led me to grow up more like a tomboy. Unlike the other girls, I didn't find much interest in all the girly things, but I would get very excited when I had to chase someone or punch a guy on his nose. I found it difficult to get along and make good friends with girls; and if at all I had girls as friends, I would then be their bouncer - I would fight for them on their behalf. And at college, I would sit in the center with all the boys around me. But during the *Healing and Deliverance Conference,* I realized that this was not God's plan, and the ministry member had to cast out the spirit of man from me. I heard myself speak like a man. I was shocked, but I knew I was in a safe place, and allowed the ministry member to lead me into deliverance.

During the sessions at the *Conference,* God also reminded me that I had seen the nakedness of my dad. We had a small rented house during my childhood and we slept in one room. Every morning I would wake up before him, and most of the time I have seen him naked since his clothes would be lying away. I hadn't realized what a great impact this had on me. I developed the nature of looking at men and unknowingly looking at their private parts. This was even without my knowledge. But when I brought this up in my ministry time I understood the root. I also used to watch pornography, and had had oral and anal sex. I had premarital relations with my husband, and he also had, had relations with other women, due to which there was a spirit of lust that had come into our life. The ministry member helped me to be released from these bondages. For the first time after the School, I felt a difference in my relationship with my husband. I felt pure.

These were the deliverances I got during the *Healing and Deliverance Conference,* post which every day has been an experience with God. I now know God and I are very close. I am a work in progress and know that the experiences I am going through are God's work in me for a higher purpose. Today, I am part of the ministry team and being used as God's channel for healing and deliverance in the lives of many. I praise and thank God that He has chosen me as worthy in His Kingdom, which is what I value the most.

TESTIMONY II

I accepted Jesus in the year 2004. But I never took my salvation seriously, until recently.

My 1st encounter with a cigarette was at the age of 8. My dad was a smoker, and as a child, I had watched him smoke and wanted to try it. So, I used to pick up the end of leftover cigarettes. Guess this held on to me until it surfaced completely at the age of 16, by which time I was a full-fledged smoker in college. Over the years there were days when I smoked over 60 cigarettes. I was ashamed of myself because I had no control over my actions. For about 10 years smoking played a big role in my life and I didn't want to quit. I was empty on the inside, and used the cigarettes to provide me comfort.

In May of 2010, there was this massive emptiness that overwhelmed me, and I felt an immense burden to go to church, to talk to someone and get my walk with God right. But there was no way I would do that. I thought, I was such a bad person, a heavy smoker and was so sure that I could and would not quit! There was no way I could talk to anyone about it. Imagine an Indian girl smoking! I waited for a while hoping that the feeling would die down, but it just increased. I thought that if I didn't find a solution to overcome this feeling, I would just die!

I came to Adonai by the end of the month (May 2010). I was sure I did not want to tell anyone what I was going through. I was an emotional wreck and I despised myself. Oh my God!!! What would they think of me?

Standing outside Pastor Victor's office, I had a million thoughts running through my head. After what seemed like a storm had passed from within me, there was this sudden calmness. A sort of 'gentle peace'. I went in to meet him and with my head hung low I said, *"I don't think I can quit, but I'll try cutting down"* - the usual dialogue from all smokers. Over the next few months, I tried all possible ways to quit smoking, but I did not succeed. Though I complained and cried about it, I was happy that there was someone here whom I could count on.

During the session on the Father's Love, something happened, and I knew that this time God had touched me. So, I went to my room, picked up my cigarettes and said, *"I know, I cannot do this with my own strength, I am weak! I have tried too many times and failed! But Lord, I trust that You will give me the strength to quit!"* All 5 cigarettes were flushed down the toilet... and I've been free ever since. God is so Faithful. How true this verse is - *Ephesians 2:8-9 - "For it is by grace you have been saved through faith and this is not from yourselves, it is the gift of God not of works, lest anyone should boast."*

CHAPTER 13

Blessings And Curses

13.1 We are Redeemed from the curse to Receive the Blessings of Abraham

(Galatians 3:13-14)
"Christ redeemed us from the curse of the law by becoming a curse for us, for it is written: Cursed is everyone who is hung on a tree." (14) He redeemed us in order that the blessing given to Abraham might come to the Gentiles through Christ Jesus, so that by faith we might receive the promise of the Spirit."

13.2 What is a Curse?

Anything that is not a blessing, is a curse. Many Christians believe that when they accept Jesus as their Saviour, the curses over their lives are automatically broken.

<u>A person living under a curse will have the following symptoms:</u>
a. Breakdown of relationships - *(Leviticus 20:6)*
b. Absence of peace - *(II Kings 9:22)*

c. Lack of success:
Many people see initial prosperity and success, but over a period of time they lose everything; they lose their position, their finances, etc...(Example : Saul - I Chronicles 10:13)

Notes:

People go through life not knowing why they keep facing such problems.
(Proverbs 26:2)
"... an undeserved curse does not come to rest."

13.3 Causes for a Curse

a. Carved Images - *(Exodus 20:3-5, Exodus 34:14, Deuteronomy 32:16, I Corinthians 10:20-21,
    II Corinthians 6:16)*
b. Witchcraft - *(Galatians 5:19-20)*

13.4 Consequences of Carved Images and Witchcraft

(Leviticus 19:31)
*"Do not turn to mediums or seek out spiritists, for you will be defiled by them. I am the LORD
your God."*

13.5 Partnership with the Devil through Occultism and Witchcraft

(Acts 19:19)
If someone is involved with any of the things listed below, ministry will be necessary.

a. <u>Fortune Telling</u>
    Ouija boards, tarot cards and any other kinds of fortune telling such as palmistry, crystal ball
    gazing and tea leaf reading.

    Isaiah 47:13
    *"All the counsel you have received has only worn you out! Let your astrologers come forward,
    those stargazers who make predictions month by month, let them save you from what is coming
    upon you. They don't have power to change the circumstances."*

b. <u>Spiritualism</u>
    The belief that the spirits of dead people can communicate with people who are still alive
    (especially via a medium). Seances and mediums, automatic writing and spiritualist healing,
    horoscopes.

Notes:

c. <u>Astrology</u>

It is the belief that the stars and planets have an influence over the behaviour and happenings in human lives. A person's character and destiny are said to be influenced by the zodiac signs. Many people plan their lives around what astrology says. It is a demonic thing that controls you. *(Isaiah 47:13)*

d. <u>Magic</u>

Black and white magic, table-lifting, levitation and casting spells.

e. <u>Mystical</u>

Transcendental meditation, astral projection, mind reading and mental telepathy.

f. <u>Religious</u>

Satanism, idol worship.

g. <u>Superstition | Vaastu</u>

The beliefs which arise from family or cultural traditions have a binding upon people's lives. These beliefs are exploited by evil spirits and can act as a curse if the superstitions are not broken. Many superstitions are to do with combating sickness or ill fortune, and are often connected with the significant times of change in people's lives, such as conception, birth, entering adulthood, puberty, marriage and death.

In many cultures, the 'evil eye' is a powerful superstition; somebody may be perceived to look at you or your child with the 'evil eye', which will bring a curse or bad fortune. Charms may be employed to ward off the effects of this superstitious evil look. Another group of superstition relates to animals and their behaviour. Eg. When a dog barks, especially in the dark, it is meant that an evil spirit is passing by.

h. <u>Charms</u>

Many people wear the signs of the zodiac or other symbols on bracelets or necklaces. Symbols of the horse shoes, etc. are hung on door posts. Frequently crosses and crucifixes are worn with exactly these motives of bringing luck. *(Ezekiel 13:20)*

Notes:

Testimonies For Blessings And Curses

TESTIMONY I

I was in my teens when someone introduced me to the *'Ouija Board'* – a board which has alphabets and numbers on it, and requires a coin and a candle which the medium uses to operate the board and invite the spirit of someone who has died. I soon mastered this just so I could show off to my friends - little did I realize what I was getting myself into.

It happened during the preparation for my 10th Grade exams. I was challenged by my sister and her friends to summon the spirit of an actress. My mother was around, and looked on curiously. Sure enough, the spirit answered my call and responded to all the questions we asked it. And what followed was both shocking and dizzying at the same time; it took us straight into another realm. This continued for four hours until I had to go for tuitions. And so, I then requested the spirit to leave. And that's when devastation struck.

On all the previous occasions, I had called the shots. But this time around, the spirit took charge. It ignored my pleas and the cries of the others present. It began to misbehave in a terrifying manner. Darkness descended into the room, and there was chaos, confusion and an ominous presence that seemed to engulf us. A girl who was present with us began to cry hysterically, and there were screams of fear. Feeling responsible, I begged it to leave. Finally, the spirit agreed, but, on one condition - I had to promise I would invite it again, which I did, even though I had no intention of keeping this promise.

Phew, I told myself, never again! But, easier said than done... by dabbling with those powers, I had enrolled myself into the kingdom of evil; something which I came to know of, only later.

My mother narrated what had happened, to an aunt who was a Believer. My aunt was very concerned, and said that we had made ourselves vulnerable to an evil spirit. I reassured her to not worry since I had no intentions of having anything to do with it.

But, it wasn't going to be so easy, as we discovered in the months that followed. Promises that are made are as binding in hell, as they are in Heaven. I had promised that evil thing I would invite it, and since I did not, it struck back.

I fell ill - dreadful diseases visited me one after the other. I found it hard to retain the food I consumed. I had excruciating headaches which couldn't be healed with any medication. I screamed all the time - there was no respite. The doctors had no idea what was happening to me. Detailed investigations revealed nothing. The best doctors gave up. Everything seemed to fail. My body just could not take it. My family was grieved. And my groaning echoed on the hospital floor. Soon, whatever I vomited was black. It felt like all was over. By now, whoever visited me would give their condolences to my parents, knowing that I was standing at the gates of death. Near and dear ones did everything possible – fasted, visited far off religious places, took me to various people who were believed to cast out evil spirits, but all this was done in vain. Nothing seemed to be working. But then Jesus broke through, My aunt (the one who had previously asked me to discontinue dabbling with the occult) visited me. She didn't look fearful like the others. Instead, she looked at me, straight into my weak and desperate eyes, and said, "This is something only The Lord Christ can combat", and added, "You are looking for life. No one who is dead can give you life. Only someone who is Alive can give life. Jesus resurrected on the 3rd day, proving He is Alive, and thus, He can give you life."

When I heard about the Resurrected Jesus, a divine ray of hope sparked within me. I invited Jesus into my life, and asked His Forgiveness, for having allowed Satan to enter my life by dabbling with the evil spirits. The wages of sin is death, but the Gift of God is Eternal Life. Within the same week, I began responding to the treatment. What a Miracle! Going further, I continued with the same medicines that were given to me earlier, but though I had not responded to them before, now, all of a sudden, the same medicines started to agree with me and work effectively in my body, and soon my body began to function without any external support. I was overjoyed to be able to stand on my feet again.

That was the turning point of my life, and since then two decades have passed. By His Grace, I am saved through Faith, that was Gifted to me, from HIM. Ever since, I have been enjoying the Blessing of an Abundant Life. My life has been a living testimony. Jesus forgave me, and also set me free from the curse and consequence of my sin.

I know I am not the product of my past, but the product of the CROSS.

TESTIMONY II

Even after my water baptism, I continued to live an ungodly life.

I was very passionate about dancing, and so, I took up Kathak, an Indian classical dance. Though I had made my terms clear to the institute that I would not participate in any chants, pujas or bowing down before any idol, I compromised when doing the "namaskar", as it was considered an essential element of the dance. Even though that inner voice kept pricking me, I suppressed it.

During my time of personal ministry, as the ministry team prayed against my involvement with classical dance, my hands became stiff, my spine went numb and I lost my posture. I also felt strong vibrations from my shoulder to my fingertips, when all of a sudden that spirit left me and I was delivered from that bondage.

TESTIMONY III

‧Even though I accepted Christ, something kept holding me back. Every time the Lord grew nearer, I would go far away from Him. I was an Indian classical dancer from the age of eight. Due to the dance I used to worship Shiva. I did not know that offering flowers and dakshina would have such an effect on me. After hearing the teaching on 'Blessings and Curses' - I renounced all forms of idol worship, and God set free of all the demons I had within me. The ministry time I had was awesome.

I am also a single mom. I became a mother when I was 19 years old, when I was forced into sexual intercourse by a friend who later abandoned me. I shifted cities to have the baby and pursue my education. Today my child is 4 years old, but during the course of those years, I underwent depression and committed a lot of sins. I kept jumping from one relationship to another, in the hope of finding a compatible partner. Also, the last relationship I had was with a satanic worshipper which held me in bondage. All this only further weighed me down.

During ministry, I dealt with all my ungodly soul ties and went to the root of the issue - my father. He used to sexually assault me, night after night, and that caused me to fear. So, the spirit of fear was in me along with the spirit of lust.

As the ministry team prayed for me, I felt so much anger within me. I felt that the spirits never wanted to leave me.

But, in the Name of Jesus, I felt every demon flee, and today I feel like a new creation. I have decided to live my life for Jesus, and to also take responsibility for my daughter.

CHAPTER 14

Generational Iniquity

The repetition of similar disorders and diseases from one generation to another is a commonly accepted phenomenon. There is a clear reason for this, if we consider the spiritual affect of sin in the generational line.

14.1 God's Plan for Blessings Through the Family

a. Parents teaching and training their children in Godly ways. *(Genesis 18:18-19, Proverbs 6:20-22, II Timothy 1:5)*

b. Spiritual inheritance of blessing. *(Deuteronomy 7:9, Psalm 103:17, Numbers 14:24)*

14.2 The Effect of Sin in the Family Line

a. God's warning. *(Exodus 20:5-7)*

b. Particular types of sin bring particular curses. e.g. sexual sin. *(Deuteronomy 23:2-3)*

c. Iniquity brings disorder to the family line. *(Lamentations 5:7-16)*

14.3 The Nature of Sin

a. Sin has a consequence. *(Romans 6:23, Galatians 6:7)*

b. Sin establishes iniquity (being out of line with God). *(Hosea 10:12-13)*

c. Iniquity is a condition of disorder which puts us outside of God's covering. *(Lamentations 5:7-8)*

Notes:

14.4 The different words used to describe the different categories of sin

a. Transgression - Deliberate breaking of laws and rules laid down by God.
b. Trespass - Going into territory or behaviour that God forbids.
c. Rebellion - Refusing to accept God's Authority.
d. Iniquity - A lawless nature; a tendency to sin that we inherited from Adam and our ancestors.

14.5 The Atonement

a. At the Cross, all our iniquities fell on Jesus. *(Isaiah 53:5-6)*
b. This truth is foreshadowed in the ritual of the Day of Atonement. *(Leviticus 16:7-10)*
    • The Sacrificial Goat - the blood sacrifice. *(Leviticus 16:15)*
    • The Scapegoat - the bearer of iniquity. *(Leviticus 16:21-22)*

14.6 Biblical Examples of the Effects of Generational Iniquity

a. <u>Sexual sin</u>
    • David - generational sexual iniquity. *(Psalm 51:5)*
    • David continues the sin in his own life. *(II Samuel)*
    • David's son Amnon continues to sin under the same generational line. *(II Sam 13:14)*

b. <u>Abuse</u>
    • Abraham fails to protect his wife Sarah. *(Genesis 12:12-13)*
    • Isaac fails to protect Rebekah. *(Genesis 26:7)*

14.7 The Family Tree

a. Recognising patterns of behaviour or disorder in the family line can help to reveal what particular iniquity might be giving the enemy authority over one's life.
b. There is an outworking of iniquity over the family line, apparently to the third and fourth generation. *(Exodus 20:5, Genesis 15:16)*

c. <u>Examples of common situations encountered</u> in ministry:
    • Infirmities such as cancer and allergies.
    • Disorders such as addictions, sexual distortions and broken marriages.
    • Patterns of control and abdication of authority.

Notes:

14.8 Was it not dealt with at our new birth?

a. There will come a time "in those day... when all know the Lord", when generational iniquity will not be visited on the children. *(Jeremiah 31:29-34)*

b. At present, we need to appropriate the atoning work of the Lord Jesus on the Cross, bearing the iniquity of man.

c. Generational iniquity, though it brings pressure, it does not excuse our own sin.

14.9 God's Solution

a. Confess the sins of our forebears. *(Nehemiah 1:5-11, 9:2, Daniel 9:3-8, Ezra 9:6-7, Levitucus 26:40)*

b. Forgive them for the effect that their sin has had in our life.

c. Repent for continuing to sin in similar ways. *(I John 1:9)*

d. Take hold of the truth that, in Christ Jesus, we are set free from the spiritual inheritance of generational iniquity visited into our lives. The ungodly line is broken. *(Galatians 3:13-14)*

e. Recognise that we are now grafted into a new spiritual family, with an inheritance of 'only blessings' in the family line. *(John 1:12)*

f. Appropriate the fullness of freedom from this bondage, by asking God to expose any demonic powers derived from this generational iniquity. Drive out these powers.

Notes:

Testimonies For
Generational Iniquity

TESTIMONY I

I was born to a Hindu family in a village. My father was an alcoholic, and was also very strict; he would beat me without any reason, and so I developed anger and hatred towards him. He was also a fearful person, and did not take up any job to take care of the family. My mother was a housewife. As a result, we lived in poverty.

Here is a bit of how my life was:
The people in my village were very superstitious. At a very young age my parents took me to a Vishnu temple, and branded me with a red hot iron, on both hands, with the image of the idol.

I was very good at studies, and was quite ambitious, but because of our financial state, found it difficult to pay for my education. And at school the teachers and students showed partiality between the rich and the poor, and this made me angry and rejected.

When I was in the 3rd std, I was introduced to the ouija board by my cousins, and thereafter continued to play with it for fun.

As I became a teenager, I developed revolutionary thoughts, got interested in naxalism, became very rebellious towards situations like injustice, inequality, partiality, poverty, etc...

At the age of 14, when I was in the 9th std, one of my teachers spoke about evil spirits, and said that we can talk to spirits and they would understand and help us. That caught my attention. From then on, I began to talk to imaginary friends and evils spirits regularly, and offered myself to them, asking them to use me in whatever way they needed. I also began to communicate with the dead and my ancestral spirits. At the same time, I began to grow very fond of horror movies, which resulted in me having nightmares everyday.

During the same time, I was sexually abused by few people. At the age of 15 (10th std), I was exposed to yoga and meditation, and soon reached a high level in yoga, hoping to get supernatural powers through it.

At this time, I started worshipping at the Iskon temples and would keep mini slokas and the bhagavathgeetha and started reading all the stories of the ramayana and mahabharatham. I did all these things because I was frustrated with the situation at home. I also got involved in all their rituals including blood sacrifices.

When I was 18 years old, I got into a relationship with a boy which led to severe depression, and began to struggle with loneliness, which led me to search the internet in hopes of finding the to key to happiness. I found studying as one of the ways to cope with my loneliness. Around this time, I was also diagnosed with hyper thyroidism.

At the same time my mother in her old age gave birth to my baby sister, and because of this our relatives treated us badly and rejected us.

In my second year of Post Graduation, a class mate from South Africa introduced me to CHRIST. I started going to church every Sunday, but I found it difficult to listen to the message preached; I would feel very sleepy and had to pinch myself to keep awake.

When I got baptized, my boyfriend left me. At this stage, I developed a migraine problem and severe depression premenstrual syndrome, and so started using homeopathic medicines.

I wanted to help my family and so I joined as a reporter cum writer in an environmental magazine, where I was exposed to communism, marxism and feminism. I used to fight for justice, and became a rebel. But, the situation at home was bad and I had to leave the job.

I got another job as a lecturer in another city. It was a private university located in the middle of the forest. I was very happy for one month and then things changed. Every night, at 12 O' Clock, I would feel some spirit come into my room and sexually abuse me, and this would go on till 3AM in the morning. From that time onwards there was a lot of change in my body - in the way I spoke, the way I walked, my eyes, etc. The staff observed these changes and told me about it. Also, because of me, others in the hostel would hear scary voices, and so they isolated me; I couldn't go out because they would treat me like a dog, and throw food at me. I used to cry a lot. I didn't know what to do.

In the same college there was a Christian teacher who called her pastor, and he told me that someone had sent 12 demons to oppress me, and they were in my body. He said he couldn't pray for me because those demons didn't allow him to pray. So, I went to another pastor, and the demons in me started to manifest. I started to lose control of my body and mind. I would hear these evil spirits asking me to go and fall in front of moving vehicles. I found it very difficult to control myself. I was all alone. I had a lot of fear. My friends took me to another pastor, who also told me similar things and asked me to resign the job saying that the place was haunted.

During this time, few people told me about the Adonai Healing and Deliverance Conference, but without listening I went to a psychiatrist instead, who gave me some medicines to sleep. So, I resigned that job. For 3 months I suffered. The medicines made me lose my emotions, and I couldn't express what I was going through. I lost my appetite for food. My condition was not good; I was unable to stand and talk and became very weak. But my father thought that I was willfully not going to work, and so blackmailed me; he wrote a suicidal note saying that my mom and I were going to be responsible for his death. When I started attending interviews, everyone rejected me because of my physical condition. Few people gave me money, to help me recover soon. But my situation only kept getting worse. And my father tortured me for money. Our neighbours felt sorry for us and gave us food.

I stopped taking my medicine, but couldn't sleep from 12 to 5AM, since I started hearing voices, like someone crying, or a man was singing. I would even see demons. At this stage I got a severe lung infection, and was diagnosed with eosinophilia. The doctor also told me that I had a split personality and that I was suffering with bipolar disorder.

I was completely isolated from people. And every day I could only sleep from 5AM to 7AM. I got another job in yet another city, but no matter where I went the demons would follow me and torment me, never allowing me to do my work.

At work, my boss began to manipulate and control me. He also took advantage of me sexually. I couldn't bear it; I cried a lot, but found that I couldn't do anything. I hated myself for all that happened. And because of what was happening I began to get tormented with sexual thoughts. So I asked a doctor for medicines to prevent these thoughts, but my boss tried preventing me from having them. I hoped his family would rescue me, but they thought I had psychological problems and started giving me alcohol to stop my crying. I didn't know how to escape.

To forget my pain I started yoga and classical dance, which only resulted in such extreme body pain that I had to crawl on the floor to move around. Doctors suspected rheumatic arthritis, but the tests came back negative. I started consuming ayurvedic medicines. In time, I began to loose control over my body and mind; my nerves would pull, I had severe headaches and my nails became like claws. Doctors said I may have to be admitted to a mental hospital.

Day by day my situation only kept getting worse. And this was when I was sent to Bangalore for a small training. I also thought this was a good opportunity to see few good doctors. And that is how I came to attend the Adonai Healing and Deliverance Conference in April.

During the sessions, I found it very difficult to sit through and every night I was still struggling; many demons would to talk to me - they cried, begged, requested, and even threatened me - they didn't want me to leave them. They told me that since we were together for 25 years, they wouldn't trouble me, and that they wouldn't let anything harm me. They also tried convincing me to not believe in Jesus. I was getting really fed up with all the struggles. I even tried to escape from this School.

But, God is Faithful. During my ministry time, JESUS delivered me from all those spirits. The following month (May) I attended the Conference again, and continued to receive Jesus' healing and deliverance.

Today, I no longer depend on any medicine. It's been more than 6 months, and all my medical reports confirm that I am perfectly fine. I no longer suffer with any issues from thyroid, migraine, lung infection, premenstrual syndrome; nothing. I am totally healed. I am no longer tormented with sexual thoughts, and don't suffer from fear or anxiety any more. I am so happy, and enjoy being in His presence. I have experienced the power of Christ that sets people free. I am in love with Christ.
Jesus has turned my tears into songs of joy.

TESTIMONY II

During ministry time, I was set free from a spirit of lust which had come down the generational line. I also walked in lust since as a child I was sexually abused, and also because of the unclean literature that was made available to me from those who had abused me. Even in my marriage, I felt something was missing. Though I have been a Christian for over 25 years, I always felt my slate was never clean; I longed to open up to someone, but was very afraid to do so. For the first time, I opened up voluntarily. After ministry, I felt a lightness in my spirit. I really look forward to enjoying the abundant life that God has in store for me.

TESTIMONY III

I was born in a traditional family to parents who were staunch Hindus. As a family, we worshipped an endless list of idols for personal favours and yet, we were not happy and lacked peace. We were extremely anxious and constantly worried about our future, and I became so depressed and lonely that I created an imaginary world around me, where everything was to my liking, and I enjoyed fantasizing about that world.

After my engineering, I started working, and through a friend, at work, I came to know about the Lord and eventually accepted Christ. But, I still lived in bondage, though I didn't understand what was happening. At night I was tormented with nightmares of snakes and other spirits, and at times could feel someone trying to choke me.

I attended the *Healing and Deliverance Conference* in April 2012. At the school, the teaching gave me an understanding that these experiences were a direct result of idol worship and the generational sins of my forefathers.

As a child:
- I was dedicated to Shiva, our family deity.
- We made offerings to snakes and sacrificed animals.
- We also practiced astrology, numerology, vaastu and many other Hindu beliefs which were all rooted in the occult.

During my time of ministry, I repented from all the rituals I was involved in, and the ministry team broke the power of darkness and its consequences over my life. That same night, I saw the spirit of Shiva leaving me in a dream. I was also set free from spirits that held me bound through astrology, numerology and superstitious beliefs. The very next morning I was baptized in the Holy Spirit and began speaking in tongues. I felt a freedom that was unknown to me earlier.

I later attended the Prayer *Ministry Seminar,* where I received more clarity about what had actually happened during the *Healing and Deliverance Conference* ministry. The spiritual realm became more real to me. I went on to join the ministry team. Today, ministering to people deepens my conviction and I'm also able to see the reality of how the spiritual realm of darkness has kept people spiritually blind and bound. My one desire is for God to use me to see other people set free. And in Him, I am complete.

CHAPTER 15

Ministry Guidelines

15.1 Introduction

All members on the Ministry Team have signed a 'Confidentiality Form', to ensure you absolute confidentiality in what you share. The objective of the Ministry Team is to make this a safe place for people to be open, so that they can receive healing and freedom in areas of their lives that have been held captive by the enemy.

James 5:15-16 (NIV)
"And the prayer offered in faith will make the sick person well; the Lord will raise him up. If he has sinned, he will be forgiven. (16) Therefore confess your sins to each other and pray for each other so that you may be healed. The prayer of a righteous man is powerful and effective."

15.2 The benefits and dynamics of ministering in pairs

a. Jesus sent out the disciples in twos; there is power when two agree. *(Luke 10:1, Matthew 18:19)*.
b. It is helpful to have one ministry team member of each sex. The member of the opposite sex should be understanding and provide security to the guest. (Sometimes there will be exceptions to this).
c. It enables the Ministry Team to test Words of Knowledge, and the other Gifts of the Spirit, before action is taken.

Notes:

d.   It provides continuity in ministry (in the event of one ministry team member being absent), and it helps the person not to become dependent on one person.

15.3   What to expect during the Ministry of Deliverance

a.   At various stages during the prayer ministry, emotional healing and deliverance may take place. Some of the manifestations may be similar to those of emotional pain, so be careful to not immediately assume that deliverance is taking place. Deliverance can also take place with no obvious manifestation.

b.   Manifestations that are commonly observed during deliverance are sudden violence, hissing, swearing, snarling and pungent smells.

c.   The obvious manifestations for you to believe you are free is a sense of lightness in your spirit: you will know that something has lifted from you.

d.   Resistance from the enemy will usually mean that the enemy's foothold (authority) has not been completely removed through confession, etc...

15.4   When demons leave, it can be sensed in the following ways:

a.   They can just lift-off with no obvious manifestations.

b.   From the throat and mouth, through deep breathing, yawning, burping, coughing, vomiting, choking, etc...

c.   Through the eyes, ears or nose.

d.   Off the top of the head.

e.   Through the feet, toes or other parts of the body.

After deliverance, ask the Holy Spirit to fill the place that has been vacated by the spirit. There is no need to fear re-invasion unless you deliberately put the 'welcome mat' down.

15.5   God's Responsibility and Our Responsibility

a.   What can we expect God to do?
   • To forgive us of all our sins - *(Psalm 103:2)*
   • Heal our body - *(Matthew 8:17)*
   • Heal our emotions - *(Isaiah 53:3)*

Notes:

- Restore the damaged will
- Heal our spirit - *(Luke 4:18)*
- Keep us from falling - *(Jude 1:24)*

b. What does God expect us to do?
   - Repent from our personal sin and ungodly reaction - *(Matthew 11:20, Mark 1:15)*
   - Renounce (cast off or disown) ungodly behaviour and wrong core beliefs.
   - Receive forgiveness and cleansing from our sin, guilt and condemnation - *(1 John 1:9)*
   - Forgive the offenders if any - *(Mark 11:25)*
   - Make the right choices - *(Deuteronomy 30:1-2)*

Notes:

Notes:

Lordship Prayer

Lord Jesus, I acknowledge my need of You and accept You as
my Saviour, my Deliverer and my Lord.

I invite You now to be the Lord, Who is the Authority over
the whole of my life.

Jesus, be the Lord of my human spirit and all my spiritual awareness
and worship.

Jesus, be the Lord of my mind, my attitudes, my thinking, my beliefs
and my imagination.

Jesus, be the Lord of my emotions and my expressions of my feelings.

Jesus, be the Lord of my will and all my decisions.

Jesus, be the Lord of my body, my physical health, my exercise,
my diet, my rest and my appearance.

Jesus, be the Lord of my sexuality and its expression. Jesus, be the
Lord of my family and all my relationships.

Jesus, be the Lord of my secular work and my Christian service.
Jesus, be the Lord of my material goods and my perceived needs.
Jesus, be the Lord of my finances.

Jesus, be the Lord of my plans, my ambitions, my future. Jesus, be the
Lord of the manner and timing of my death.

Thank You that Your Blood was shed,
that I might be free from the consequences of my sin, and that
my name is written in the Book of Life.

In Jesus' Name, Amen.

Selected Bibliography

- Horrobin, Peter J. Healing through Deliverance. Ben Publishing: India, 2004.
- Seamands, David A. Healing for Damaged Emotions. David C. Cook: Colorado Springs, 1991.
- MacDonald, Gordon. Rebuilding your broken world. Thomas Nelson Publishers: Tennessee, 1988.

Recommended Reading

- Bevere, John. Bait of Satan. Charisma House: Florida, 2004.
- Bevere, John. Under Cover. Harper Collins: New York, 2001.
- Seamands, David A. Healing for Damaged Emotions. David C. Cook: Colorado Springs, 1991.
- D'Monte, Victor. Satan and his kingdom - Exposed! Bangalore, 2018.